To Dorothy
with all best wishes
and thanks for your
loyal support of   Colby
Church music   Smith Ms

Sincerely

Thomas Brahms

TO JACK E. BOWMAN (1927-1972)

who served as a member of the music faculty of Ricks College, and through whose efforts and encouragement this second printing is accomplished.

*"With malice toward none;
with charity for all . . ."*
Abraham Lincoln

Orientation
for Interpreting

MOZART'S
Piano Sonatas

Orientation

for Interpreting

MOZART'S

Piano Sonatas

By

THOMAS RICHNER, Ed.D.

BUREAU OF PUBLICATIONS
Teachers College, Columbia University
New York, 1953

To Dora Zaslavsky,

through whose guidance and inspiration I have discovered true musical values

Allegro maestoso

K. 310

*True genius without heart is a thing of naught—for not
great understanding alone, not imagination, nor both together make genius—Love! Love! that is the soul of genius!*

—GOTTFRIED VON JACQUIN
(from Mozart's autograph album)

ACKNOWLEDGMENTS

In the preparation of this book I have been given invaluable assistance by mentors and friends. I am deeply grateful to the members of my advisory committee—Professor Raymond Burrows,* Professor Lilla Belle Pitts and Professor James L. Mursell—for their individual and collective guidance, scholarly criticism, and consistent patience. And to Noel Straus, Dora Zaslavsky, and Joseph Raymond I owe warm thanks for their encouragement and helpful suggestions.

I am indebted also to various authorities on Mozart for many of the insights presented here, and to their publishers for permission to quote from their works. A book from which I have quoted extensively, with the kind permission of the author and the publishers, is Emily Anderson's complete translation of the *Letters of Mozart and His Family* (Macmillan & Co., Ltd., London, 1938). And I owe thanks also to the publishers of the following valuable works: *Mozart —His Character, His Work*, by Alfred Einstein (Oxford University Press, London, 1945); Leopold Mozart's *Treatise on the Fundamental Principles of Violin Playing*, translated by Editha Knocker and with a Preface by Alfred Einstein (Oxford University Press, London, 1948); *Ornamentation in J. S. Bach's Organ Works*, by Putnam Aldrich (Coleman-Ross Co., Inc., New York, 1950); *The Symphonies of Mozart*, by Georges de Saint-Foix (Alfred A. Knopf, Inc., New York, 1949); *The Literature of the Piano*, by Ernest Hutcheson (Alfred A. Knopf, Inc., 1948);

* Died May 31, 1952.

ix

Mozart and the Sonata Form, by Raymond J. Tobin (William Reeves, London, 1916); *The Sonata: Its Form and Meaning,* by Helena F. Marks (William Reeves, London, 1921); *Lessons in Music Form,* by Percy Goetschius (Oliver Ditson Co., Bryn Mawr, 1904); *Mozart: The Man and His Works,* by W. J. Turner (Alfred A. Knopf, New York, 1938); *Music in Western Civilization,* by Paul Henry Lang (W. W. Norton & Co., Inc., New York, 1941); *Mozart's Piano Concertos,* by C. M. Girdlestone (Cassell & Co., Ltd., London, and University of Oklahoma Press, Norman, 1948); *The Organ Student's Gradus ad Parnassum,* by Caspar Koch (J. Fischer & Bro., New York, 1945); *A Companion to Mozart's Piano Concertos,* by Arthur Hutchings (Oxford University Press, London, 1948); and *Lectures on Musical Analysis,* by Henry C. Banister (George Bell & Sons, Ltd., London, 1902).

THOMAS RICHNER

CONTENTS

PART ONE *Orientation*

PART ONE *Orientation*

One

INTRODUCTION

A strange paradox exists concerning the musical literature of the eighteenth and nineteenth centuries. It has become traditional in the pianistic development of a student that the compositions of Bach, Scarlatti, Clementi, and Haydn serve as a technical training ground for the young artist rather than as material for profound emotional self-discovery and expression. There is a widespread impression that eighteenth century musical literature should be studied in *preparation* for the freer and more obviously "expressive" music of Chopin, Liszt, and Brahms, rather than as the full flowering of a rich and powerful expressive language in its own right.

That this tendency has included the sonatas of Mozart is not surprising. Their comparatively narrow range up and down the keyboard, their lack of wide intervals and large, full chords, bring some of them easily within the grasp of a small, undeveloped hand. The conciseness of their form and the pristine clarity of their detailed harmonic language permit easy analysis by even elementary theory students. And yet, within the terse and forthright structure of his sonata form, Mozart has devised some of his most lyric, subtle, and profound utterances—all of which are accentuated in poignancy by their deceptive simplicity.

It is the emotional depth, the wealth of imagination, the humor, and the pathos of Mozart's sonatas which many

3

teachers overlook or minimize when they assign these works to immature musical aspirants. It is these qualities which are so lacking in the majority of interpretations of Mozart heard today. The ostensible fault of such performances is that the patent objective is not the message of the music, but the ability to traverse the notes as delicately or as rapidly as possible.

This study, by contrast, is not primarily concerned with technical aspects of the sonatas but with presenting a faithful revelation of Mozart's deeply conceived intentions. The ideas expressed here are the fruit of many years of intensive study of the works involved. While it is clearly impossible to reduce such a discussion to coldly objective assertions concerning the subtle values of interpretation, an attempt has been made to index and to highlight the essence of Mozart's creations. Working conscientiously beyond the realm of this basic exposition of Mozart's piano sonatas, the student may be better enabled to understand the distinctive genius of that great composer. The discussion is couched in terms of principles and illustrative examples, thus enabling the earnest seeker to use imagination and creative thinking in terms of his own background. To provide a routine formula for dealing with the intangible elements of expression and meanings in Mozart's music would be untrue to the spirit of his art.

Two

THE INFLUENCE OF
CONTEMPORARY COMPOSERS

The interpreter seeking to give Mozart's piano works faithful and authentic performance needs some understanding of their historical background, one of the most important features of which is the direct influence on Mozart of other composers of his day. While it is not the purpose of this chapter to exhaust the research on these composers, those influences most clearly discernible in Mozart's piano music will be considered here.

Leopold Mozart

The world owes to Leopold Mozart—the father of Wolfgang Amadeus Mozart—a great debt of gratitude. Without his unceasing efforts in training and encouraging his son, we might never have had the masterpieces that we cherish today.

Leopold recognized his crucial responsibility as the father of a genius. With his pedagogical background and his clear insight into human nature, he used laudable wisdom in guiding his son. Instead of employing his own compositions as a didactic model, he assembled works of Telemann, Bach (Karl Philipp Emanuel), Hasse, Kirchhoff, and others—works of far better taste than those of young Wolfgang's contemporaries. There were abundant popular compositions available, but Leopold took pains to make certain that these works were not to be found in the Mozart home.

Emulating the examples his father had painstakingly accumulated, the child composed his first little pieces—promisingly articulate in structure, although naive in style—with exquisite taste and feeling. His discrimination and his adherence to certain principles never wavered, even though as a result of his extensive travels in Italy, France, England, and Germany, he surely came into contact with music both good and bad of his contemporaries. His powers of selective inattention (resistance to that which he did not "feel" —including most of his father's compositions) give one cause to believe that his immaculate taste was uncanny, or inborn—the ineffable x quantity which is divinely bestowed upon genius and genius alone.

Although a fair proportion of Leopold's compositions were shallow, insipid, uninspired, and somewhat "popular," Wolfgang often was touched by them. In a letter to his father (Vienna, 1783), Mozart wrote:

When the weather gets warmer, please make a search in the attic under the roof and send us some of your own church music. You have no reason whatever to be ashamed of it.[1]

Wolfgang held his father in high esteem as a teacher. On October 16, 1777, he wrote to his father from Augsburg:

It is true that she has not yet had a really good teacher, and if she stays in Munich she will never, never become what her father is so anxious that she should be; and that is, a first rate performer on the clavier. If she comes to Papa at Salzburg, her gain will be twofold; both in musical knowledge and intelligence, which is not exactly her strong point at present.[2]

Leopold was a Salzburg composer, whereas Wolfgang was a universal genius. Leopold must have sensed that he himself did not possess the necessary spark, because he

---

[1] Emily Anderson, *Letters of Mozart and His Family* (1938), III, 1259.
[2] Anderson, *op. cit.*, II, 471.

eventually turned completely to pursuits other than pure composition and concert work. One of the more important of these activities was teaching, in which, as has been indicated, he was inspiring.

This point has been amply documented. Lang gives a clear illustration:

> The most lasting influence, however, emanated from the child's father. Leopold Mozart (1719–1787) was an excellent musician, a noted violinist, and a respected composer. A man of education, he was the author of a *Versuch,* in this case dealing with the playing of the violin, a work which, appearing in the year of Wolfgang's birth, remained a highly esteemed violin method for almost a century. The father's excellent pedagogical insight can be seen in the remarkably rounded musical literature he gave his children, drawing on French, Italian, and German compositions both southern and northern.[3]

In summation, the first major influence on Mozart was Leopold's care and nurture of his son's divine gift. Alfred Einstein, observing the relationship between father and son, put it somewhat less positively: "Leopold shines in the reflected glory of his son's halo, without which he would have remained in obscurity."[4]

Johann Eckardt

While in Brussels, Mozart became acquainted with the sonatas of Johann Gottfried Eckardt, famous pianist and composer who settled in Paris in 1758 and who took from his teacher, Karl Philipp Emanuel Bach, the new sonata form and contributed greatly to its thematic development and to the idea of three movements. Eckardt made extensive use of the "Alberti bass" which Mozart later employed in his sonatas. The Alberti bass, so named after Domenico Alberti's development and use of it, consists of breaking the

---

[3] Paul Henry Lang, *Music in Western Civilization* (1941), p. 637.
[4] Alfred Einstein, in Preface: Leopold Mozart, *A Treatise on the Fundamental Principles of Violin Playing,* tr. by Editha Knocker (1948), p. vii.

notes of a chord conveniently for the left hand.* Eckardt's
contributions to sonata form and his use of the Alberti bass
have considerable importance as factors influencing Mozart's
development.

Johann Schobert

Mozart was influenced perhaps more by Johann Schobert,
French harpsichord player and composer, than by Eckardt,
although the latter was the more learned and scholastic.
Schobert, too, according to Wyzewa and Saint-Foix, was
influenced by the French tradition. His works had grace
and sensitiveness which made them attractive to the young
and impressionable Mozart.

Although Mozart was affected by Schobert in his development of the form of his sonatas, he was still more per-
ceptibly influenced in his use of minor keys for pathetic,
tragic, and emotional expression, and of *tempo rubato*. In
another chapter of this study, Mozart's choice of tonalities
and harmonies is considered in detail. For example, the
effects of his turning to A minor in the "Tragic" Sonata
(K. 310), and his use of the *pathétique* key, C minor (K.
457), are of sufficient interest to merit separate consideration.

Turner also affirms Schobert's influence upon Mozart,
asserting:

Mozart's whole social outlook was entirely different from his father's
and the difference in temperament is strikingly shown even when
as an eight-year old child in Paris in 1764 he was attracted to the

* For example:

music of Schobert by an affinity of nature, whereas his father, Leopold, did not approve of Schobert, describing him as "low and not at all what he should be."[5]

Despite Leopold's somewhat uncomplimentary attitude toward Schobert, the latter exerted an influence upon Wolfgang which, in the final tally, may be considered in an affirmative light.

Johann Christian Bach

A really great influence on the young Mozart which one can readily discern in many of his early works is that of Johann Christian Bach—"the English Bach," as he was often called. The "English" or "London" Bach was the "black sheep" (according to the admirers of the other Bachs) because he differed greatly from his father, Johann Sebastian, and from his brother, Karl Philipp Emanuel. He was completely "Italian" in his approach.[6] It was in the combination of the German and Italian styles that Mozart felt a deep kinship with Johann Christian Bach. Perhaps no writer, with the possible exception of Joseph Haydn, influenced Mozart more.

In a letter of February 28, 1778, Mozart wrote:

For practice I have also set to music the aria *"Non so d'onde viene,"* etc. which has been so beautifully composed by Bach. Just because I know Bach's setting so well and like it so much, and because it is always ringing in my ears, I wish to try and see whether in spite of all this I could not write an aria totally unlike his. And, indeed, mine does not resemble his in the very least.[7]

A letter written in August of the same year gives further clues concerning influences in Mozart's musical tastes:

[5] W. J. Turner, *Mozart: The Man and His Works* (c1938), p. 60.

[6] "Italian" signifies lightness, *buffo* character, sweetness of melody, and a *galant,* essentially lyrical instrumental style. [See E. J. Dent, *Mozart's Operas* (1947), p. 16; or Einstein, *Mozart—His Character, His Work* (1945), p. 117.]

[7] Anderson, *op. cit.,* II, 736.

Mr. Bach from London has been here for the last fortnight. He is going to write a French opera, and has only come to hear the singers. He will then go back to London and compose the opera, after which he will return here to see it staged. You can easily imagine his delight and mine at meeting again; perhaps his delight may not have been quite as sincere as mine—but one must admit that he is an honourable man and willing to do justice to others. I love him (as you know) and respect him with all my heart; and as for him, there is no doubt but that he has praised me warmly, not only to my face, but to others also, and in all seriousness—not in the exaggerated manner which some affect.[8]

In the Saint-Foix study of the symphonies of Mozart, one again sees reference to Mozart's unfailing adherence to the principles of Johann Christian Bach. Saint-Foix, who is considered one of the leading authorities on Mozart, declares:

But despite these factors of musical transformation, Mozart remains obstinately attached to practices that his London master had himself never pursued with a like persistency: during the whole of 1767—a year of study and reflection—the characteristic Italianisms of Christian Bach are retained in all his instrumental movements; that is, neither development or a return of the principal subject in the tonic key.[9]

One of the themes in Johann Christian Bach's Quintet in D appears in a Mozart Rondo (Late Period, K. 485):

Joh. C. Bach, Op. XI, No. 6

And this passage from one of Johann Christian's six clavier

[8] Anderson, *op. cit.*, II, 900.
[9] Georges de Saint-Foix, *The Symphonies of Mozart* (1949), p. 11.

Joh. C. Bach, Op. XVII, No. 4

sonatas was evidently in Mozart's mind when he wrote:

Allegro   K. 333

These examples serve to spotlight Johann Christian's influence upon Mozart. The influence is indeed prominent and could be extensively documented by further examples. But attention must turn to a fifth contemporary influence upon Mozart.

Michael Haydn

After Johann Christian Bach, Mozart was influenced more by the Haydn brothers than by any of his other contemporaries. Joseph Haydn especially had an important part to play in Mozart's life. Michael, the younger brother, was director of the Archiepiscopal Orchestra in Salzburg, and later concertmaster as well as organist at the Cathedral.

Saint-Foix's perception of the influence of the Haydn upon Mozart is quote-worthy:

> What is the impulse behind the birth of these four grand sym-phonies? One can see in them a sort of "sublimation" of the com-positions of the two Haydns—for, since his return to Salzburg Mozart felt himself more and more attracted by the work of his confrere and friend Michael Haydn, whom of course he very quickly surpassed in originality and intensity of expression. Mozart was indebted to Michael Haydn for that ideal poetic beauty of certain of the andantes, a kind of reverie that often attained the summit of his artistic crea-tion. For Michael Haydn, despite his native indolence, had the soul of a poet, which revealed itself, not only in some admirable sacred music, but also in his symphonies and chamber music, by melodies of an infinite tenderness, and dances of a quality and harmonization intimately "Mozartian."[10]

Joseph Haydn

As Einstein puts it, "The contemporary master from whom Mozart learned most, after Johann Christian Bach, was the elder of the brothers Haydn—Joseph."[11]

There is a reasonable certainty that Mozart must have heard some of Haydn's symphonies during his early visit to Vienna in 1768. This experience, coupled with the hear-ing of Haydn's six quartets, Op. 20, made a deep impression on the young Wolfgang; so much so that he imitated Haydn, writing two sets of six quartets of his own—one (K. 168–173) in 1773, and another (K. 387, 421, 428, 458, 464, 465) in 1782–86. Otto Jahn writes:

> The most charming instance of Mozart's reverence and love for Joseph Haydn is the dedicatory epistle wherein he offers him his six quartets as the fruit of long and painful study inspired by his example, as a father intrusts his children to a tried and valued friend, con-fident of his protection and indulgence towards them. These expres-sions of reverence came from the very depths of Mozart's heart: to a friend who made some remark on the dedication he answered: "It

---

[10] Saint-Foix, *op. cit.*, p. 48.
[11] Einstein, *Mozart—His Character, His Work* (1945), p. 126.

was due from me, for it was from Haydn that I learned how quartets should be written."[12]

What a lucid and eloquent acknowledgment of admiration and influence! Such an expression could emerge only from the soul of one who is an artist in his own right and who needs not seek the artificial and short-lived comfort of pretending total originality of idea and form. This is but another facet of Wolfgang Mozart's true spirit.

It was through the influence of Joseph Haydn that Mozart became aware of his own genius. Haydn was a conscious musical revolutionary. His long residence in a rural atmosphere brought forth new ideas which were gently charged with a tinge of the iconoclastic—ideas which rebelled against the *galant* style of the times. Always original, his individuality in creative activity developed in spite of the criticisms of his dubious and less gifted contemporaries. Fortunately, the quality of this originality was profoundly understood by Mozart.

Haydn's piano sonatas, like his quartets and symphonies, also served as models for Mozart. Haydn wrote six sonatas in 1773 which could easily have served this purpose. Again, Einstein indicates a case in point:

Thus, for the Sonata in F (K. 280) a sonata by Haydn in the same key served as model; and in the Sonata in E-Flat (K. 282) not only is the finale quite Haydnish, but the irregularity and the subjectivity shown in the sequence of the movements reflect Haydn's influence. . . . And in the B-Flat Major Sonata (K. 281), of which the first two movements seem more like Haydn than Haydn himself, we are suddenly faced, in the Finale, with Mozart at his most characteristic and individual.[13]

Haydn was partly responsible for Mozart's awareness of and growth in counterpoint. In his quartets were several fugues; and two of Mozart's early quartets ended, like

[12] Otto Jahn, *The Life of Mozart* (1882), II, 348.
[13] Einstein, *Mozart—His Character, His Work* (1945), pp. 241–242.

Haydn's, with fugues. But it was later, through the private concerts of Baron Gottfried van Swieten, that Wolfgang became acquainted with the contrapuntal works of Handel and of the great Johann Sebastian Bach.

It is impossible to assess the immense service that Haydn rendered music. It was left for him to establish the sonata and symphonic forms as we know them today. Although attempts were made by such writers as Karl Philipp Emanuel Bach to find originality in this new form, there is no parallel to Haydn.

Hutcheson further substantiates Haydn's great service to music:

Many of us are still apt, perhaps, to think of Haydn principally as an amiable, rather unsophisticated forerunner of Mozart and Beethoven. This is a complete misconception of his genius, only to be accounted for by the fact that the effortlessness and spontaneity of his writing easily delude us into an impression of naïveté. In truth, he was a greater originator than either Mozart or Beethoven: he created the sonata form, they adopted it, expanded it, and experimented with it.[14]

Thus, it is seen, Mozart made use of basic conceptions from other highly endowed musical minds of his period, and with the spark of his own native genius gave them new, undreamed-of contexts which must endure so long as printed matter itself survives. His flexibly observant disposition enabled him to recognize that he was not the only genius of his time, and that his contemporaries—of varying musical statures—created material which merited his admiring and most serious contemplation.

Johann Sebastian Bach

It was through Baron van Swieten that Mozart discovered Johann Sebastian Bach. Mozart came into contact with the Baron (who was then President of the Education Com-

---

[14] Ernest Hutcheson, *The Literature of the Piano* (1948), p. 62.

mission) in 1781, and became a faithful visitor at the musical gatherings held every Sunday morning in his home. Introduced to the music of Johann Sebastian Bach by Frederick the Great, van Swieten had been led by his intense interest to obtain not only the printed works of the great master, but also manuscript copies of *The Well-Tempered Clavier* and of the preludes, fugues, and trios for organ— compositions unknown in Vienna at that time. Mozart's creative activity was stirred, even revolutionized, by contact with this contrapuntal music of the highest order.

These musical gatherings are mentioned in a letter Mozart wrote to his father on April 10, 1782:

I have been intending to ask you, when you return the rondo, to enclose with it Handel's six fugues and Eberlin's toccatas and fugues. I go every Sunday at twelve o'clock to Baron van Swieten, where nothing is played but Handel and Bach. I am collecting at the moment the fugues of Bach—not only of Sebastian, but also of Emanuel and Friedemann.[15]

An enthusiastic letter to his sister on April 20, 1782, had more to say about the effects of his first hearings of Bach's works:

I send you herewith a prelude and a three-part fugue [3] [[3] K. 394, Fantasy and Fugue in C major.]. . . . My dear Constanze is really the cause of this fugue's coming into the world. Baron vàn Swieten, to whom I go every Sunday, gave me all the works of Handel and Sebastian Bach to take home with me (after I had played them to him). When Constanze heard the fugues, she absolutely fell in love with them. Now she will listen to nothing but fugues, and particularly (in this kind of composition) the works of Handel and Bach. Well, as she had often heard me play fugues out of my head, she asked me if I had ever written any down, and when I said I had not, she scolded me roundly for not recording some of my compositions in this most artistic and beautiful of all musical forms, and never ceased to entreat me until I wrote down a fugue for her. . . . In time, and when I have a favourable opportunity, I intend to compose five more [1] [[1] K. App. 39 and K. App. 40, both unfinished, were

[15] Anderson, *op. cit.,* III, 1192.

Mozart's attempt to carry out this plan.] and then present them to Baron van Swieten, whose collection of good music, though small in quantity, is great in quality.[16]

It is of interest to note that Mozart arranged a number of Johann Sebastian Bach's fugues (from *The Well-Tempered Clavier, The Art of Fugue,* and the Organ Sonata No. 11), as well as one from Wilhelm Friedemann Bach, for van Swieten's string ensemble. His experience in mastering the difficulties of counterpoint served only to enrich his imagination and to perfect his attainments.

While one finds only isolated instances of contrapuntal writing in the piano sonatas, it is remarkable that all of the contrapuntal passages are completely effortless, seeming to fit perfectly into the contexture. Their presence makes for a beautifying of the structure and is not, by any means, an end in itself. Mozart's eloquent maintenance of perspective as he easily relegates complex technical matters of this type to a secondary place is noteworthy—and not un-Bachlike.

Especially contrapuntal is the first movement of the Sonata in F Major (K. 533), and the opening of the B Flat Major (K. 498a). While the D Major (K. 576) is not contrapuntal in a strict sense, it indeed shows the effect of contrapuntal study, as does the middle section of the last movement of the B Flat Sonata (K. 570). It is in these later sonatas of the Vienna period that we feel the part-writing emerging to a position of primary importance. One can say, with Einstein: "Mozart prefers to hide his counterpoint, to conceal his 'art'; it must not appear as artificiality. This is part of his nature."[17]

It is the duty of the performer of Mozart's piano works to study not only the Fugue for Two Pianos in C Minor (K. 426), and the Fantasy and Fugue in C Major (K. 394), but also the fugue in the Suite in the Style of Handel (K. 399). These numbers will contribute a great deal

[16] *Ibid.,* III, 1193–1194.
[17] Einstein, *Mozart—His Character, His Work* (1945), p. 154.

toward preparing the student for the more contrapuntal compositions, such as the Mass in C Minor (K. 427), the *Litaniae* (K. 243), the *Kyrie* in D Minor (K. 341), the *Kyrie* in C (K. 323), the Mass in C Major (K. 337), the *Vesperae de Dominica* (K. 321), the *Vesperae solennes* (K. 339), the *Graduale* (K. 273), the *Missa brevis* (K. 258), and the contrapuntal devices of the spring quartets and quintets. To the uninitiated student of piano, this may seem like a large undertaking; but it is vital to the goal of fully appreciating Mozart's deeper intentions. To resort to analogy, it is to be compared with a mining engineer's need to be thoroughly aware of the earth's substructures, and of the direction, breadth, and continuity of mineral veins, if his labors are to bring fruit.

The breadth, depth, and continuity of structures in Johann Sebastian Bach's massive contribution to the field have left an indelible impression upon Mozart's art.

Although this survey of contemporary influences upon Mozart is by no means exhaustive, it nevertheless traces the more readily discernible elements in his works. The influence of George Frederick Handel, while important to the period generally, has not been considered here because it was exerted principally, for Mozart, in the opera.

A second factor of far-reaching consequences in the formulation of a comprehensive perspective for Mozart's works is the piano of his time. This topic is treated in the forthcoming chapter.

Three

PIANOS
IN MOZART'S TIME

Basic to the understanding and interpretation of Mozart's
piano sonatas is a knowledge of the mechanical character-
istics of the piano of his time. It will be recalled that
Mozart wrote for the same instrument Beethoven and
Chopin wrote for. But it was not so powerful in its tone-
producing qualities as is the present grand piano. "The only
works," according to Einstein, "that can have been conceived and written for harpsichord are the early concerto
arrangements after Johann Christian Bach and minor
'French' composers (K. 107, and K. 37, 39, 40, 41)."[1]

In the Mozart household there was at least one piano
made by Franz Jacob Späth. When the instrument of the
Augsburg builder, Johann Andreas Stein, became known,
this became at once Mozart's favorite piano. His predilec-
tions in this direction are seen in a letter addressed to his
father on October 17, 1777:

This time I shall begin at once with Stein's pianofortes. Before I
had seen any of his make, Späth's claviers had always been my favour-
ites. But now I much prefer Stein's, for they damp ever so much
better than the Regensburg instruments. When I strike hard, I can
keep my finger on the note or raise it, but the sound ceases the
moment I have produced it; in whatever way I touch the keys, the

---

[1] Alfred Einstein, *Mozart—His Character, His Work* (1945), p. 237.

tone is always even. It never jars, it is never stronger or weaker or entirely absent; in a word, it is always even. It is true that he does not sell a pianoforte of this kind for less than three hundred gulden, but the trouble and the labor that Stein puts into the making of it cannot be paid for. His instruments have this splendid advantage over others, that they are made with escape action. Only one maker in a hundred bothers about this. But without an escapement it is impossible to avoid jangling and vibration after the note is struck. When you touch the keys, the hammers fall back again the moment after they have struck the strings, whether you hold down the keys or release them.[2]

Since Mozart was one of the first real pianoforte virtuosos of his time, the world is greatly indebted to him for the part he played in bringing about the fuller flowering of this instrument. It must be remembered that the piano in Mozart's time was new and was used for the most part by amateurs. In the middle of the eighteenth century it was most often used in combination with strings and other instruments, as accompanying *basso-continuo*. Subsequently the piano became more independent, as in the many "violin and piano sonatas" which were essentially piano sonatas written with violin obligatos. Mozart's B Flat Sonata (K. 570), today considered complete as a piano composition, is an excellent example.

There have been several reproductions of the piano of Mozart's day. Probably among the most important of these replicas is the instrument built by John Challis of Ypsilanti, Michigan. This piano is used by the well-known specialist of eighteenth century music, Ralph Kirkpatrick, in his New York recitals of Mozart's piano works. Having heard this instrument on various occasions, the writer would venture to say that the greatest difference between this instrument and the piano of today lies in the former's greater variation of colorings—granted that its dynamic range is smaller.

The *una corda* tone of Mozart's piano could easily have been a real one-string tone, as the name implies. In contrast

[2] Emily Anderson, *Letters of Mozart and His Family* (1938), II, 478.

to this, the modern piano utilizes two strings when the *una corda* pedal is depressed. This explains the almost imperceptible change in actual color from the *tre corde* (utilizing all three strings).

The general *tre corde* tone of the piano in Mozart's time was exuberantly rich in overtones. It achieved a brilliant, almost harpsichord, effect. Yet the *una corda* produced an entirely different color—sweet and ethereal. The color contrasts in the instrument may have been somewhat greater in this respect than the contrasts afforded by the mechanics of the modern piano.[3]

The need for understanding the nature of the piano in Mozart's time becomes apparent. First of all, the performer of Mozart's works today must select an instrument which offers great dynamic contrasts. Secondly, the piano must possess a rich singing tone. This is, indeed, a difficult order. So few pianos have both a truly *dolce* tone for *una corda* passages, and at the same time a crystal-clear brilliance for negotiating the passages which by their very nature insist upon the freshening breath of contrast.

Even when such an instrument is found, the actual contrasts must be further emphasized by masterful touches of the performer, rather than minimized by reliance solely upon the mechanical possibilities of the instrument itself.

[3] The writer, during a visit to Salzburg, Austria, studied the Walther piano, now preserved in the Mozart Museum. While it was, indeed, limited, having two octaves less than the modern instrument, there was a damper pedal operated by the knees, and a knob on the front-piece just above the keys. This knob controlled a felt damper between the hammer and string, creating an effect much like the *una corda*.

In Vienna, the writer found one of the Beethoven pianos in excellent condition. It was enlightening to discover a piano with five pedals! (1) the damper pedal for elevating the dampers; (2) a pedal placing felt between hammer and string; (3) a pedal for placing parchment over the strings to produce a harpsichordal sound; (4) a pedal for sustaining the lower half of the keyboard (similar to modern sustaining pedal, but only sustaining the entire section instead of individual notes); (5) the *una corda* pedal, with a stop on the right-hand side of the keyboard to produce either *una corda* or *due corde*.

Thus, there is demanded of the faithful performer of Mozart a technical mastery of a wide variety of tonal effects, which depends in turn particularly on the careful balance and control of weight and pure finger activity.

It is almost certain that Mozart used a five-pedal piano (see page 20, note 3). This piano was much ornamented with attachments. (Modern pianos are, in contrast, notably simple to control.) One may easily imagine the *Rondo alla Turca* (in the Sonata in A Major, K. 331) played w the Janissary attachment (a device—operated by a special foot-pedal—for playing a drum and triangle).[4]

Clearly, a considerable amount of mechanical *savoir-faire* was entailed in performing on the piano in Mozart's time: not infrequently, the better musicians had a thorough knowledge of the mechanics of the instruments they were playing. A case in point is Nannette, daughter of J. Andreas Stein, the piano builder. She was a practical piano maker, and at the same time a pianist of noteworthy talent. She habitually tuned her own piano before giving a public concert.[5] Perpetuating the tradition, she married A. Streicher, whose talents were similar to her own, and together they improved the Viennese grand piano.

Another piano typical of those used in Mozart's time is the grand piano which the Brothers Erard made for Napoleon I in 1801. It operated on the Stein principle, but also shows the point of departure from which Erard subsequently developed his own action. This piano has the five or six pedals customary in Austrian and German instruments of that time. Going from left to right, the pedals are "piano," shifting the action; "bassoon," a parchment slip which contacts the strings for some three octaves; the "damper"; and the "piano celeste" (muting by thin cloth). Next, for Janissary music, came the drum and triangle de-

[4] The existence of the drum effect suggests a militant spirit congenial to Mozart.

[5] This subject is treated in Ernst Pauer's *Dictionary of Pianists* (1895), in the article on Stein.

vices: the drumstick struck the underside of the instrument. Another piano pedal was not uncommon: a sourdine that muted the strings with leather, and was evolved from a late version of the harpsichord. The contemporary English grand pianos used two pedals, but the "piano" pedal was controlled by a stop in the block, which gave the player a choice of one string or two, according to the effect the player wished to achieve. The damper, operated by a divided foot pedal, gave the option of raising the dampers in bass or treble or both together. This arrangement of the pedals was used until about the year 1830. The shifting pedal is attributed to the inventiveness of J. Andreas Stein; he termed it a *Spinetchen*. It has been conjectured that the pedal was so called because it was *una corda,* as in the spinet —operating one string only to each note.[6]

The foregoing observations have highlighted mechanical aspects of the piano in Mozart's time. Besides this type of instrument, what other factors helped account for the distinctive qualities of his compositions—and in turn bear upon a faithful modern interpretation of the sonatas?

In answer to this question, there are three main factors: his choice of tonalities and harmonies, his ornamentation, and his own notions of interpreting piano works. These aspects are considered, in the order mentioned, in the succeeding three chapters.

[6] See A. J. Hipkins, *A Description and History of the Pianoforte* (1896), p. 106.

Four

MOZART'S TONALITIES
AND HARMONIES

Tradition and Choice of Tonalities

In Chapter Two, the influence on Mozart of such composers as Johann Eckardt, Johann Schobert, Johann Christian Bach, Michael and Joseph Haydn, and Johann Sebastian Bach has been outlined: Mozart was firmly anchored in tradition—in his selection and use of tonalities no less than in other important ways. He inherited much of the *galant* musical tradition, including a stylistic custom of stressing a melody with a homophonic accompaniment. The material was often trivial, even banal in its prettiness; yet Mozart, with his subtle use of polyphony, his genius and exquisite innate taste, took such simple ideas and gave them depth and an immaculate being. Similarly, he chose as his points of departure, with few exceptions, what may be called the "simple" keys, or "neutral" tonalities, and used them with unique restraint and ingenuity to arrive at profound and often delightfully unexpected expressions. He was moreover frugal in "spending" keys, which, it would seem, he regarded as one of the precious currencies of musical expression: he selected from the possible variety of keys even less freely than did most of the composers who influenced his growth. This unusual restraint in the use of tonalities is an important aspect of the purity of Mozart's works and of the superlatively expressive quality of their relatively "simple" and undramatic language; and it is at once a part of his musical inheritance and a manifestation of the genius which transcended it.

Changes from the Original Tonality

Mozart's orientation within an original key served to strengthen his tonal unity. Haydn, for instance, would wander off into strange keys,[1] using enharmonic devices in long passages, which resulted even in changing the key signature. This, in turn, eventually weakened the tonality of the structure. Mozart, on the other hand, always treated modulation and related keys with the utmost discrimination, never going into a strange key merely for the sake of tonal variety or originality. It is the writer's conviction, matured by years of study and performance of the sonatas, that for expressive purposes Mozart was meticulous in his choice of keys and chords.

Remote Tonalities

In the piano sonatas, as well as in the symphonies, operas, and chamber music, Mozart dealt usually in the realm of the more conventional, or "neutral,"[2] keys such as C, G, D, F, B flat, and E flat. In only three instances does one

[1] Hutcheson asserts: ". . . Haydn's range of keys was far wider than that of Mozart, whose sonatas and concertos rarely venture as far as signatures of three sharps or flats, whereas Haydn is undaunted by tonalities like A flat, D flat, and C sharp major and minor. He is equally bold in modulation and in direct leaps from key to key by simply moving a semitone up or down, as Beethoven afterwards loved to do. In sufficient proof of this harmonic daring, I need only refer to the first of the thirty-four sonatas, with its three movements in E flat, E major [sic] and E flat. In the first movement he introduces his second theme in the conventional dominant, B flat, but in the development section he springs surprises on us. Twice he comes to a pause on a G major triad, thence proceeding to entrances of the second theme, first, with happy effect, in C major and then, most astonishingly, in the utterly remote key of E major, eventually stealing back to E flat for the recapitulation by gliding chromatically from the dominant seventh of B minor to that of E flat major. The whole passage merits close study." [Ernest Hutcheson, *The Literature of the Piano* (1948), p. 62.]

[2] By the term "neutral" is meant those *major* keys with few sharps and flats. A minor, for the present study, is regarded as a "tragic" key. Other "remote" keys are F sharp, E flat minor, C sharp major.

find the sonatas written in other keys—keys which may be regarded as "remote" keys.

A MINOR: *The Tragic Key.* The Sonata in A Minor (K. 310) is one of Mozart's most dramatic works. It was conceived in a dark and somber mood. Mozart wrote it out in the spring of 1778—one of the low points in his life. He had entered upon a journey from Mannheim to Paris unwillingly, because it separated him from Aloysia Weber, of whom he thought constantly—to the point that he could not concentrate on his musical endeavors. He detested Paris, its "artificial atmosphere," and the people with whom he had to deal, including Friedrich Melchior Grimm, the patron whom his father had trusted to guide Mozart's Parisian career.

When one is acquainted with this report of the conditions under which the "Tragic" A Minor Sonata was composed, there remains little doubt as to its deeper meaning in terms of Mozart's life.[3] It seems logical to reason that Mozart attached to this key a special significance consonant with his troubled mind at the time.

C MINOR: *The "Pathétique" Key.* In the A Minor Sonata (K. 310) Mozart uses the key to reflect a dark, tragic mood. Similarly, in the C Minor Sonata (K. 457) Mozart uses the key as an expression of emotional tone best characterized as *pathétique.* This dramatic work prepares the path for Beethoven's "Pathétique" Sonata (Op. 13) and his Symphony in C Minor, No. 5, with its classic "fate" motive. Mozart's instructions for performing this sonata (published later with the C Minor Fantasy, K. 475) have

---

[3] Girdlestone substantiates this view concerning the background of the Sonata referred to: "The fine A Minor Sonata, K. 310, composed most probably in Paris, contains in its andante an almost literal quotation from Schobert's Op. XVII. Mozart, who assimilated so many and such diverse influences, took from them only what suited his nature, and if this sudden appearance of the minor is a widespread device at this time, it corresponds nevertheless to his unstable temperament which passed without transition from laughter to tears and bordered on sadness at its merriest moments. The angel of sorrow was always watching within, ready to unveil its face." [C. M. Girdlestone, *Mozart's Piano Concertos* (1948), p. 111.]

been lost. While there are differences of opinion, the consensus seems to be that this sonata should not be performed
with the fantasy.[4] The sonata was written in October, 1784,
almost eight months before the fantasy, which was written
May 20, 1785. The fantasy is so powerful in its ideas,
modulations, and structure, that it destroys to some extent
the effectiveness of the intensity in the earlier work when
it is played immediately before. Either work can stand
alone, needing no contrast with the other for added intensity.

In the final, as well as in the first, movement of the sonata,
there is a sense of demanding, dramatic power. The lovely
Adagio in the tranquil key of E flat major forms the needed
contrast between the stormy corner movements. The "fate"
motive is predominant in the last movement. This sonata
is discussed in greater detail in the analytical section of
this study.

A MAJOR: *The Key for Brilliance.* The remaining less
neutral key, A major, is utilized in all its wealth and beauty
in the A Major Sonata (K. 331), with the theme and variations for the first movement. Like many other Mozart
works, it is marked by a deceptive simplicity, and paradoxically is one of the most difficult to interpret faithfully. This
sonata is a favorite with music lovers, and has given many
people their first impression of Mozart; it is unfortunate
that it has been so often misinterpreted.

The variations of this sonata are a complement to the
variations of the Dürnitz Sonata (D major, K. 284).
Whereas the style of the earlier sonata is a revelation of
emotional beauty, unity and brilliance, the A Major Sonata

---

[4] Shedlock remarks that the unity of character and feeling between the two
no doubt led to their juxtaposition. [J. S. Shedlock, *The Pianoforte Sonata*
(1895), p. 125.]

Jahn indicates: "It [the Fantasy in C Minor, K. 475] was composed May 20,
1785, and published by Mozart, together with the Sonata in C Minor, K.
457, as Op. 11. [Otto Jahn, *The Life of Mozart* (1882), II, 449.]

Hutcheson feels they should be played together: ". . . Mozart's own title
proves that he regarded them as a single work. While it is permissible to
play each separately, the spiritual affinity is obvious. Together they con-
stitute Mozart's magnum opus for piano solo." [Hutcheson, *op. cit.,* p. 73.]

is greater in intensity. Mozart has separated the variations from the *Rondo alla Turca* with a lovely French form of minuet *(Menuetto)*. In the last movement of the Violin Concerto in A Major (K. 219), written in 1775, Mozart employed the "Turkish" style in an episode.[5] He probably had this in mind when composing the last movement of the piano sonata in A major. The "Turkish" element was not new with either of these works, inasmuch as he had used it earlier in a ballet, "Le Gelosie del Serraglio," which he composed in 1773 in Milan for his opera *Lucio Silla.*

Neutral Tonalities

Mozart chose the neutral keys for the other piano sonatas: C, G, D, F, B flat, and E flat. Although the works are oriented in such keys, this does not mean that they are less inspired, or colorless. Quite the reverse: when Mozart does achieve a momentary contrast to the established key, the effect is doubly eloquent.

In examining the developmental section of the *Andante* movement from the G Major Sonata (K. 283) one finds that it is among Mozart's most serene movements. Yet a figuration based on nothing more spectacular than a diminished seventh chord (measure 15, and the C sharp in measure 16) achieves great intensity of effect, in this neutral key, with wonderfully simple treatment. It is intensified by exact imitation in the right hand, heard again with embellishments, and once more repeated in the right hand.

Chordal Structuring

Mozart exercised as much care in his choice of chords within a key as he did in his choice of the key itself.[6] His judicious use of the diminished chord to suggest unrest—a

---

5 "Turkish" style: strongly rhythmic march style, using or suggesting triangle, cymbals, and bass drums, for an effect like that of the Janissary bands.
6 In the discussion of the *Sinfonia Concertante* for violin and viola (K. 364), Saint-Foix says: ". . . we do not know the occasion that called forth

particular facet of his use of the minor for deeply serious, tragic, or *pathétique* intent—was as significant in his music as his melodic conceptions.

One of the most striking instances of the power vested in Mozart's use of chords is found in the slow movement of the C Major Sonata K. 330. This *Andante cantabile* is in F major; its trio is introduced in a *pianissimo* tonic minor, ending with a pronounced discord achieved by the suspension of E natural (measure 41) through the F minor chord. This is resolved at the last moment, which yields a delayed climax of memorable restraint.

Chord choices in the C Minor Sonata (K. 457) accomplish a tremendous surge of pathos. This effect is demonstrated clearly by the implied keys in the *a piacere* section (measures 230–244) of the last movement. After the II₇, the diminished chord resolves into the II₇ in F minor. Then the V₆/₅ is suspended into F minor. Finally, the V changes to VII₇ in G minor before a return is made to the original C minor! What a masterful invention!

This sonata (K. 457) epitomizes Mozart's exquisite taste in structuring chords so as to express most adequately his musical conceptions. The excellence of his judgment in this process constitutes, in part, his genius.

Leaving the subject of tonalities and harmonies we shall consider next Mozart's use of ornamentation.

this great work. It is noble and passionate, and it is not difficult to see in it an anticipation of several of the works of the master's maturity in the same key, E flat, which are analogous in feeling with this work—*for different keys represented for Mozart particular modes of poetic expression.* The plaintive and somber andante is a sort of elegy, the sordins, as it were, stifling the sobs; it is one of those painful, even poignant moments that are far from rare in Mozart." [Georges de Saint-Foix, *The Symphonies of Mozart* (1949), p. 82. Italics mine.]

Five

ORNAMENTATION

Inconsistency of the Editions

It is lamentable that many editions of the Mozart piano sonatas are inconsistent in their interpretation of ornaments, in terms of the composer's original intentions. Although the earnest student will undoubtedly use more than one edition, the confusion may even be heightened because of a lack of consistency within the various editions.[1]

It is indeed difficult to establish rigid rules of ornamentation for the piano works of Mozart. Ultimately, the spirit

---

[1] This inconsistency is understandable, considering that even the authorities disagree.

Aldrich: ". . . the last half of the eighteenth century is precisely the period of the most rapid changes in both the composition and performance of music . . . changes which brought about the disintegration of the Baroque ideals and the formation of the Classic style of Mozart, Haydn, and Beethoven." [Putnam Aldrich, *Ornamentation in J. S. Bach's Organ Works* (1950), p. 2.] C. Koch also is aware of this dilemma: "The somewhat violent shift in style and taste which marked the middle of the eighteenth century was a vital factor in obscuring for us the compositional and interpretive methods of the preceding era." [Caspar Koch, *The Organ Student's Gradus Ad Parnassum* (1945), p. xi.]

On the other hand, Dannreuther feels there is no reason for debate and affirms: "There is no evidence which could lead one to believe that W. A. Mozart departed from his father's practice as regards the rendering of ornaments. Reference to Leopold Mozart's book [see bibliography] will suffice to decide questions that may arise." [Edward Dannreuther, *Musical Ornamentation* (1893–95), II, 95.]

of the music is the only true guide the interpreter may
follow.[2]

There are, however, several general rules to keep in mind
as aids to correct ornamentation. The ornaments most often
used in the sonatas and most likely to be misunderstood
(largely through copyists' mistakes and engravers' technical errors) are (1) the appoggiatura, (2) the trill, and
(3) the turn.

Ornaments Often Misinterpreted

THE APPOGGIATURA. This ornament has become con-
fused with the acciaccatura, since the two are similarly
written—each as a small note slurred to the following one.
They are, however, entirely different in purpose.

The acciaccatura (from the Italian word meaning "crush
together," and written as a small note with a stroke across
the stem) is improperly indicated in Mozart's sonatas where
the appoggiatura should be indicated. Better known as the
"grace note" and called "passing appoggiatura" by Leopold
Mozart,[3] the acciaccatura is played as quickly as possible,
not changing the value of the note it embellishes.

[2] It is regrettable that Hutchings refused to touch upon the subject of ornamentation in his otherwise valuable treatment of Mozart's piano concertos.
He slights this vital point, saying: "It may be remarked that I have said
nothing about (*a*) ornaments in performance, or (*b*) the soloist's occasional
or permanent function as continuo or thorough-bass player. These are still
matters to be debated by textual scholars, but they *are* still debatable and also,
so far as the performer is concerned, of small importance. . . . We can enter
into the musical world of Mozart without the aid of singer or player who,
in the matter of ornaments, tries to reproduce the practices of Mozart's day."
[Arthur Hutchings, *A Companion to Mozart's Piano Concertos* (1950), p.
206.]

[3] Leopold Mozart remarks: "There are both descending and ascending
appoggiature, which, however, are divided into accentuated appoggiature
and passing appoggiature. The descending appoggiature are the most natural,
for according to the most correct rules of composition they possess the true
nature of an appoggiatura. For example:

The descending appoggiature are of two kinds: namely, the Long and the
and the Short. Of the long there are two kinds, of which one is longer than
the other. If the appoggiatura stands before a crotchet [quarter note], quaver
[eighth note], or semiquaver [sixteenth note], it is played as a long appoggiatura and is worth half of the value of the note following it. The appog-

The appoggiatura is an ornamental note, foreign to the harmony with which it is sounded, which possesses definite duration in time value, and which is in most instances dynamically more important than the note upon which it leans. There were in Mozart's time rules regarding its time value. One rule—often disregarded then and now, but used and considered basic by the present writer—was that the appoggiatura took half the value of the note it preceded. If the note it preceded was dotted, then it took two-thirds of the value assigned to that note. Early editions differ in the value *indicated* for the appoggiatura itself: some were written as eighths, some as sixteenths; and some appear as thirty-seconds, which were not always half the value of the embellished note (hence the reason for some flexibility in the rule). The performer must exercise judgment and taste in departing from the rule for musical reasons.

THE TRILL. A mistaken idea about the trill is that it is

giatura is therefore sustained the length of time equivalent to half the note and is slurred smoothly on to it. . . . The second kind of the long appoggiatura which may be called the longer appoggiature are found firstly before dotted notes; secondly before minims [half notes] if they occur at the beginning of a bar in 3/4 time; or if in 2/4 time or 4/4 time only one, or at the most two occur, of which one is marked with an appoggiatura. In such cases the appoggiatura is held longer. . . .

Now there be also short appoggiature with which the stress falls not on the appoggiatura but on the principal note. The short appoggiatura is made as rapidly as possible and is not attacked strongly, but quite softly. The short appoggiatura is used: (1) when several minims follow each other, of which each is marked with a little appoggiatura note; (2) or if at times only one minim be present which, however, occurs in such a passage as is imitated immediately by a second voice in the fourth above, or in the fifth below; (3) or else if it be foreseen that the regular harmony, and therefore also the ear of the listener, would be offended by the use of a long appoggiatura; (4) and finally, if in an allegro or other playful tempo, notes descend in consecutive degrees or even in thirds, each being preceded by an appoggiatura; in which case the appoggiatura is played quickly in order not to rob the piece of its liveliness by the long-sustained appoggiatura. . . .

. . . the passing appoggiature, intermediate appoggiature, and other similar ornamentations in which the stress falls on the principal note, . . . [are] rarely or never indicated by the composer. . . . [The performer] must know how to apply [these] in the right place according to his own sound judgement." [Leopold Mozart, English translation by E. Knocker, *A Treatise on the Fundamental Principles of Violin Playing* (1948), pp. 167–177.]

merely a trick for prolonging the sound.[4] Trills, properly conceived, enhance and enliven melodies. In the sonatas of Mozart they are indispensable.[5]

Although various editions of the Mozart sonatas differ, today most authorities agree that the trill begins on the upper auxiliary. It is played on the beat with emphasis on the note which is dissonant to the harmony. The performer may use (*a*) the simple cadence trill,* (*b*) the cadence trill with termination,** or (*c*) in special cases, the "turn."

The speed of the trill is determined purely by the context of the music it is embellishing. Leopold Mozart clarifies this:

> The trill can be divided into four species according to its speed: namely into slow, medium, rapid, and accelerating. The slow is used in sad and slow pieces; the medium in pieces which have a lively but yet a moderate and gentle tempo, the rapid in pieces which are very lively and full of spirit and movement, and finally the accelerating trill is used mostly in cadenzas. . . . The trill must above all things not be played too rapidly, for otherwise it becomes unintelligible and bleating, or a so-called "Goat's trill."[6]

THE TURN. Occasionally, Mozart used the turn as an embellishment in its own right. At other times, it was used as a substitute for the short trill. When there is not time to trill, a turn is appropriate. Since there is no fixed rule in this case, it must be left to the judgment of the discriminat-

---

[4] For further clarification of this point, see C. P. E. Bach, *Essay on the True Art of Playing Keyboard Instruments* (1949), p. 99.

[5] "The purpose of trills, mordents, and other embellishments was *not* to prolong the sonority produced by instruments that were incapable of sustaining tone, such as the harpsichord and spinet. The presence of the embellishments in organ compositions should be enough to discredit this fallacy, but some commentators have put it down to a confusion of keyboard styles on the part of the composers." [Aldrich, *op. cit.*, p. 10.]

[6] Mozart, *op. cit.*, p. 189.

*[Simple cadence trill]   **[Cadence trill with termination]

ing performer to use the proper embellishment in its correct musical context.[7]

The turn consists of four notes only. It begins with the appoggiatura above the main note and generally is played in an even rhythm, the exception being when the main note is a dotted note. (See the example.[8])

The placing of the turn over the dotted note is to be interpreted in such a manner that the last note of the turn should coincide with the dot. In this case, the figure will end with two notes of equal value.

It must be granted that ornamentation demands, in a sense, a micromathematical precision. Paradoxically, at the same time, the writer cannot venture into the realm of dogmatic rules for interpreting Mozart's plastic tonal creations. Certain principles have been set forth so that they are reasonably specific but at the same time not rigid. To interpret faithfully Mozart's ornamentations, the performer

---

[7] Aldrich gives an excellent account of this substitution: "The trill with termination and the turn may then be regarded as functionally synonymous, just as the plain trill and the appoggiatura from above are synonymous. A comparison of various manuscript sources of Bach's organ works reveals the fact that copyists often vacillated between the sign for the turn and for the trill in corresponding phrases of the same piece, and that what is indicated as a turn in one copy frequently appears as a trill in another. These considerations, together with Bach's own carelessness with regard to the signs of the *agréments,* suffice to justify the performer's substitution of a turn for a trill with termination whenever the former seems more suitable to the tempo." [Aldrich, *op. cit.,* p. 52.] Although Aldrich is writing with Bach's organ works in mind, the same idea applies to Mozart's ornamentations.

[8] Example reprinted from Aldrich, *op. cit.,* p. 52, by permission of Coleman-Ross Co., Inc.

must strive to find a balance between rigid rules and a re-laxed, flexible conception of that which the composer origi-nally intended. The modern performer's large task is to fashion those threads left him by biographers into the fabric Mozart created.

To assist in this task, biographers have gleaned from Mozart's letters many specific ideas and suggestions for in-terpreting his music. These notions are brought into focus in the chapter that follows.

Six

MOZART'S IDEAS
ON PIANO PERFORMANCE

Mozart's ideas regarding piano performance can be reconstructed to a substantial degree on the basis of fragmentary information gathered from his letters. Constituting a large part of this data are his notions relative to (a) the hands and wrists, (b) speed and its resultant inaccuracies, (c) body weight, (d) good taste and restraint, (e) ease of execution, (f) freedom from affectation, (g) rhythmic precision, (h) the *tempo rubato,* and (i) "singing tone." All of these aspects of interpretation are crucial to the forthcoming analysis of two representative piano sonatas from each of the three periods of Mozart's life.

The Hands and Wrists

Mozart stressed the importance of *quiet hands and supple wrists.* The performer of Mozart's piano works must acquire the art of finger dexterity, which is contingent upon a separation of the arm weight from the fingers. Passage work in the sonatas must "flow like oil."[1]

Mozart admonished his sister in a letter of June 7, 1783:

Well, I have a few words to say to my sister about Clementi's sonatas. Everyone who either hears them or plays them must feel

[1] This is Emily Anderson's translation of Mozart's expressive phrase. [Emily Anderson, *Letters of Mozart and His Family* (1938), II, 496.]

that as compositions they are worthless. They contain no remarkable or striking passages except those in sixths and octaves. And I implore my sister not to practise these passages too much, so that she may not spoil her quiet, even touch and that her hand may not lose its natural lightness, flexibility and smooth rapidity.[2]

Speed and Its Resultant Inaccuracies

One of the main stumbling blocks in performances in this day of haste is fast playing, against which one cannot warn himself too frequently. In the letter above, Mozart continued:

For after all what is to be gained by it? Supposing that you do play sixths and octaves with the utmost velocity (which no one can accomplish, not even Clementi) you only produce an atrocious chopping effect and nothing else whatever.[3]

Leopold Mozart shared this view of the evils of excessive speed, as seen in this letter to his son (January 29, 1778):

Indeed I am no lover of excessively rapid passages, where you have to produce the notes with the half tone of the violin and, so to speak, only touch the fiddle with the bow and almost play in the air.[4]

Mozart was distressed when he heard playing that was too fast, resulting in slovenliness and bungling. In a letter to his father, he spoke of the playing of Herr Vogler:

I should mention that before dinner he had scrambled through my concerto at sight (the one which the daughter of the house plays—written for Countess Lützow). He took the first movement prestissimo—the Andante allegro and the Rondo even more prestissimo. . . .

Well, you may easily imagine that it was unendurable. At the same time I could not bring myself to say to him, *"Far too quick!"* Besides, it is much easier to play a thing quickly than slowly: in difficult passages you can leave out a few notes without anyone noticing it. But is that beautiful music? In rapid playing the right and left hands can be changed without anyone seeing or hearing it; but is

2 *Ibid.,* III, 1267.
3 *Ibid.*
4 *Ibid.,* II, 672.

that beautiful? And wherein consists the art of playing prima vista? In this; in playing the piece in the time in which it ought to be played and in playing all the notes, appoggiaturas and so forth, exactly as they are written and with the appropriate expression and taste, so that you might suppose that the performer had composed it himself.[5]

Body Weight

Mozart was quiet at the keyboard, but would use his entire body weight if the occasion demanded. Barrington indicates that Mozart, when young, could and did rise, both figuratively and literally, to such occasions!

The boy again looked back with much archness and began five or six lines of a jargon recitative proper to precede a "Song of Anger." This lasted also about the same time [as] the "Song of Love." And in the middle of it he had worked himself up to such a pitch that he beat his harpsichord like a person possessed, rising sometimes in his chair.[6]

Studying the various biographies of Mozart, one gains the impression that when more years had cooled the ardor of his blood, Mozart became less disposed to depart from his chair and customarily maintained a position of serenity at the keyboard, bringing body weight to bear only upon the more insistent passages.

Good Taste and Restraint

Although Mozart felt that music must be expressed with the greatest of passion if it were needed, he never exceeded the limits of good taste. He indicated his feeling on this subject in a letter to his father, as well as in four succeeding letters to other persons:

For just as a man in such a towering rage [Osmin's rage in Act II] oversteps all the bounds of order, moderation and propriety and com-

[5] *Ibid.*, II, 662.
[6] Daines Barrington, "Account of a Very Remarkable Young Musician," *Philosophical Transactions of the Royal Society* Vol. XL (1770), p. 626.

pletely forgets himself, so must the music too forget itself. But as passions, whether violent or not, must never be expressed in such a way as to excite disgust, . . . music, even in the most terrible situations, must never offend the ear, but must please the hearer . . . [and] must never cease to be *music* . . .[7] (To his father on September 26, 1781. Vienna: He is discussing the music of his opera, *Die Entführung aus dem Serail.*)

You see, therefore, that what is important is that he should play with taste, feeling and brilliancy; . . .[8] (January 8, 1783)

We now have here the famous Strinasacchi from Mantua, a very good violinist. She has a great deal of taste and feeling in her playing.[9] (April 24, 1784)

I must write in a hurry. Herr Richter, the clavier-player, is making a tour on his way back to Holland, his native country. . . . He plays well so far as execution goes, but, as you will discover when you hear him, he is too rough and laboured and entirely devoid of taste and feeling.[10] (April 28, 1784)

I know what Mysliwecek's sonatas are like, for I played them at Munich. They are quite easy and pleasing to the ear. I should advise my sister, to whom I send my most humble greetings, to play them with plenty of expression, taste, and fire and to learn them by heart. For they are sonatas which are bound to please everyone, which are easy to memorise and very effective when played with the proper precision.[11] (November 13, 1777)

The above excerpts serve to indicate that Mozart was constantly concerned with a high standard of taste in pianistic performances. Central to these letters are the concepts of taste, feeling, and, to a lesser extent, brilliancy.

Ease of Execution

Mozart abhorred a laborious approach to any performance on any instrument. This attitude is defined sharply in a letter addressed to his father (November 22, 1777). It was written after Mozart heard Herr Franzl play a violin concerto.

7 Anderson, *op. cit.*, III, 1144.   10 *Ibid.*, III, 1305.
8 *Ibid.*, III, 1246.   11 *Ibid.*, II, 544.
9 *Ibid.*, III, 1304.

You know that I am no great lover of difficulties. He plays difficult things, but his hearers are not aware that they are difficult; they think that they could at once do the same themselves. That is real playing. He has too a most beautiful, round tone. He never misses a note, you can hear everything. It is all clear cut. He has a beautiful staccato, played with a single bowing, up or down; and I have never heard anyone play a double trill as he does. In a word, in my opinion, he is no wizard, but a very sound fiddler.[12]

His judgment of Herr Richter in this respect was quite different, as shown in the letter of April 28, 1784:

He plays well so far as execution goes, but, as you will discover, . . . he is . . . [forced]. When I played to him he stared all the time at my fingers and kept on saying: "Good God! How hard I work and sweat—and yet win no applause—and to you, my friend, it is all child's play." "Yes," I replied, "I too had to work hard, so as to not have to work hard any longer."[13]

In a letter of October 23, 1777, he described his performance of his Strassburg concerto as "going like oil." In the same note, Mozart referred to his organ playing, which evidently he had mastered:

Then the others whispered to the Dean that he should just hear me play something in the organ style. . . . The Dean was absolutely staggered. "Why, it's simply phenomenal, that's all I can say," he said. "I should never have believed what I have heard. You are a first-rate fellow. My Abbot told me, it is true, that he had never in his life heard anyone play the organ so smoothly and so soundly."[14]

Freedom from Affectation

Mozart avoided affectation. This is a laudable trait for any performer. But it does not imply that the performer must sit back and let melodies issue forth as though they were the result of some heaven-sent inspiration he may feel he possesses. Too many times first-rate performers have

[12] *Ibid.*, II, 565.
[13] *Ibid.*, III, 1305.
[14] *Ibid.*, II, 495.

succumbed to this temptation simply because the mechanics of playing did not demand any notable expenditure of energy. There is indeed much difference between an affectation and a movement or gesture employed tastefully to emphasize intensity, phrasing, or timing.

In an excruciatingly humorous letter (October 23, 1777), Mozart described the unfortunate affectations of Herr Stein's daughter, Maria, when she played:

Anyone who sees and hears her play and can keep from laughing, must, like her father, be made of stone. For instead of sitting in the middle of the clavier, she sits right up opposite the treble, as it gives her more chance of flopping about and making grimaces. She rolls her eyes and smirks. When a passage is repeated, she plays it more slowly the second time. If it has to be played a third time then she plays it even more slowly. When a passage is being played, the arm must be raised as high as possible, and according as the notes in the passage are stressed, the arm, not the fingers, must do this, and that too with great emphasis in a heavy and clumsy manner. But the best joke of all is that when she comes to a passage which ought to flow like oil and which necessitates a change of finger, she does not bother her head about it, but when the moment arrives, she just leaves out the notes, raises her hand and starts off again quite comfortably—a method by which she is much more likely to strike a wrong note, which often produces a curious effect.[15]

This letter is quoted at some length because it strikes the writer as one of the best single examples of Mozart's sharply critical attitude toward typical pianistic tics, gyrations, unnecessary movements, and grimaces.

Rhythmic Precision[16]

Mozart insisted upon playing in strict time. The phrase "strict time," however, does not mean metronomic time. It should be interpreted to mean keeping a steady pulse from a *rhythmic* point of view. In a later part of the letter quoted above, Mozart said, "Everyone is amazed that I

15 *Ibid.,* II, 496.
16 See also the paragraph on Speed and Its Resultant Inaccuracies.

can always keep strict time." He went on to deplore Maria's seeming unawareness of, or lack of sensitivity in, rhythmic precision:

> . . . she will never acquire the most essential, the most difficult and the chief requisite in music, which is time, because from her earliest years she has done her utmost not to play in time. Herr Stein and I discussed this point for two hours at least and I have almost converted him, for he now asks my advice on everything.[17]

Tempo Rubato

Contrary to current beliefs, Mozart used a type of *tempo rubato*. It is interesting to note that immediately after stating, "Everyone is amazed that I can always keep strict time" (see paragraph above), Mozart went on to say, in the same letter: "What these people cannot grasp is that in *tempo rubato* in an *Adagio,* the left hand should go on playing in strict time. With them, the left hand always follows suit."

This would seem to indicate that the use of the *rubato* in Mozart's time was definitely circumscribed within rhythmic limits.

"Singing Tone"

Mozart was keenly aware of tonal values in playing piano works. Variation of tonal qualities is a key to the heart of his piano sonatas. Without this flexibility, this heart could not pulsate its vital message into the body of Mozart's music.

Once, after his playing of his Strassburg concerto had been enthusiastically received, he wrote happily, "Everyone praised my beautiful, pure tone."[18]

That he expected the tonal dynamics of his compositions to be performed in accordance with his indications is evi-

---

[17] Anderson, *op. cit.,* II, 497.
[18] *Ibid.,* II, 495.

dent in this letter to his father (November 14, 1777, Mannheim) :

As soon as I can, I shall have the sonata which I have written for Mlle. Cannabich copied out on small paper and shall send it to my sister. . . . The Andante will give us most trouble, for it is full of expression and must be played accurately and with the exact shades of forte and piano, precisely as they are marked.[19]

Mozart's insistence upon the singing tone is documented further in the Vienna letter to his father, wherein he laments, "The young lady is a fright, but plays enchantingly, though in cantabile playing she has not got the real delicate singing style. She clips everything."[20]

The foregoing generalizations, highlighting Mozart's attitudes toward playing, indicate to the teacher and student ways for improving performances of his works. Gleaned from the master's original words, they should be constantly before the pianist as he ventures into the world of Mozart's sonatas.

The remaining two chapters, or Part Two of the study, are devoted to an overview of the three periods of Mozart's sonatas, and to an analysis of representative sonatas (two from each period).

[19] *Ibid.*, II, 548.
[20] *Ibid.*, III, 1112.

PART TWO *Interpretation*

Seven

THE THREE PERIODS:
A PERSPECTIVE

For the purpose of analysis, Mozart's life is arbitrarily divided into three periods: the Early, Middle, and Late periods.[1] The present chapter gives an overview of all the piano sonatas except those that have been selected for detailed analysis in Chapter Eight.

THE EARLY PERIOD

` ι his nineteenth year, Mozart wrote six piano sonatas (K. 279–284). Five were composed in Salzburg in 1774. The sixth was written in Munich in 1775—commissioned by a nobleman, Baron Thaddäus von Dürnitz, who never paid for it.

These early sonatas reflect the influences of the contemporaries of Mozart mentioned in the second chapter. The F Major (K. 280), the B Flat (K. 281), and the E Flat (K. 282) are particularly reminiscent of Haydn's piano sonatas. The G Major (K. 283) and the D Major (K. 284) are by far the most Mozartean, and perhaps the most distinguished, of this group of early sonatas, and have

---

[1] Early Period: Salzburg, 1774–75.
Middle Period: Mannheim–Paris, 1777–78.
Late Period: Vienna, 1784–89.

therefore been selected, as representative of the first period, for detailed interpretive analysis in Chapter Eight.

Sonata in C Major (K. 279, Summer, 1774)

FIRST MOVEMENT *(Allegro)*. The first sonata of the series is interesting for its improvisational character. The first movement is characterized chiefly by a free-fantasia style; this is especially applicable to the G minor section (measures 39–57).

SECOND MOVEMENT *(Andante)*. This movement is notably "Italian" in character, and unusual in that it is written in unabridged sonata-form with a free-fantasia development, as exemplified in measures 28–42.

THIRD MOVEMENT *(Allegro)*. This movement is dominantly contrapuntal in feeling. It is written in sonata form, rather than in the usual rondo form.

Sonata in F Major (K. 280, Autumn, 1774)

It is a safe conjecture that a Sonata in F by Haydn served as a model for this charming work.

FIRST MOVEMENT *(Allegro assai)*. This segment of the work begins with four chords conceived in an orchestral manner and defining at the outset the tonic key. There is a free-fantasia development (measures 57–82), as in the C Major Sonata (K. 279).

SECOND MOVEMENT *(Adagio)*. This movement is written in the tonic minor. The six-eight rhythm, sicilienne in character, could have been inspired by a movement from the String Quartet, Op. 20, No. 5, of Joseph Haydn.

THIRD MOVEMENT *(Presto)*. This section is written in three-eight tempo, and possesses a four-bar rhythm. Clearly, it represents one of Mozart's gayest moods.

Sonata in B Flat (K. 281, Autumn, 1774)

FIRST MOVEMENT *(Allegro)*. In this work, the first two movements are again in the Haydn style. The first movement begins with a right-hand trill on the first beat, followed by triplets. It is not only good taste to play the trill also in triplets: the ornamentation then serves as thematic material, thereby strengthening the intensity of the first motive. The trill in the last beat of measure 23 may be played as a turn.[2]

SECOND MOVEMENT *(Andante amoroso).* This slow movement is aptly described by Tobin in his valuable contribution to the interpretation of Mozart's sonatas:

> To a certain extent this little movement reflects the atmosphere of stilted formality which characterized the eighteenth century; and yet the music can only be described as unpretentious and refreshing. Within these two short pages many points may be observed which rival in charm of outline and wealth of detail some quaint and delightfully irregular example of the potter's art.[3]

THIRD MOVEMENT *(Allegro).* The last movement is the first real departure from the Haydn and Christian Bach influence. Upon this point the authorities agree. Einstein asserts:

> If the date of this rondo, with its air of a modest concerto and its melodic grace, were not so definitely fixed, we should certainly place it ten years later, in the Vienna period.[4]

Tobin shares this enthusiasm:

> This is a great movement—one that is calculated to put to confusion those who declare that the modern rondo-sonata form had its origin in Beethoven.[5]

Sonata in E Flat Major (K. 282, Winter, 1774)

FIRST MOVEMENT *(Adagio).* This initial movement and that of the A Major Sonata (K. 331) are the only ones which depart from the usual sonata form.[6]

---

[2] See Chapter Five, pp. 31–33 (The Trill and The Turn).
[3] J. Raymond Tobin, *Mozart and the Sonata Form* (1916), p. 38.
[4] Alfred Einstein, *Mozart—His Character, His Work* (1945), p. 242.
[5] Tobin, *op. cit.,* pp. 39–43.
[6] See, for instance, A. J. Goodrich, *Complete Musical Analysis,* (1889), p. 23.

SECOND MOVEMENT. This section is comprised of two *Menuettos,* whose exquisite charm and simplicity are seldom paralleled in other piano works. The second minuet may appropriately be called the trio.

THIRD MOVEMENT *(Allegro).* The last movement, instead of following the rondo form, is sonata-allegro. Although it consists of but two pages in most editions, it is rich in development; and the choice of tonalities is unusual. Modulations into F minor, B flat minor, and C minor denote a return to the Haydn influence.

With the foregoing concise presentations of Mozart's Early Period sonatas, the backdrop is set for a more detailed exposition or analysis, in Chapter Eight, of the G Major (K. 283) and the D Major (K. 284), both of which so clearly delineate the composer's inspired conception of melodic line, rhythm, and harmony.

THE MIDDLE PERIOD

Between the autumn of 1777 and the summer of 1778, Mozart wrote seven new piano sonatas (K. 309–311, 330–333). This outpouring of ideas is framed into what the writer terms the Middle Period of Mozart's career as a composer of piano sonatas. Since two of the sonatas (K. 309 and K. 311) were written in Mannheim, and the others conceived in Paris, this period is also known as the Mannheim–Paris Period. Of the two Mannheim sonatas, there is more knowledge (through the Mozart letters) of the C Major (K. 309). Therefore, this sonata has been selected for detailed analysis in Chapter Eight, as has the C Major (K. 330) of the Paris period. Since the tragic A Minor Sonata (K. 310) and the brilliant A Major (K. 331) have been analyzed for their emotional content in Chapter Four (pp. 28 and 30), their form alone will be outlined here.

Sonata in A Minor (K. 310, Summer, 1778)

FIRST MOVEMENT (*Allegro maestoso*). This movement
is in sonata form. The first theme is eight bars long, of
which the first four measures are written on the tonic pedal
point. The termination of the subject and the beginning of
the bridge passage produce an overlapping transition.

The second theme in C major is approached through the
tonic minor of its own key. This is rather unusual for
Mozart's time. And the development, too, is revolutionary,
particularly as regards key selection: opening in C major,
modulating to F major with indecision between the keys
of D minor and F major. An ascending chromatic run
joins the development and the recapitulation.

In the recapitulation, after the first theme has been faithfully stated, there is an allusion to it again in measures
88–103. On this occasion, the theme is enunciated by the
bass. The second subject is in the tonic minor.

SECOND MOVEMENT (*Andante cantabile con espressione*).
This movement is also in sonata form. As in the tempestu-
ous C Minor Sonata (K. 457), this movement begins con-
solingly, but the development readily initiates a free fantasia with tremendous agitation which prophesies the great
C Minor Fantasia (K. 475).

THIRD MOVEMENT (*Presto*). This movement, in rondo
form, begins also on the tonic pedal, as in the first movement. Unity of ideas such as are found in this example
substantially indicate that this sonata was conceived as a
whole before Mozart wrote it out. Rarely can one find a
purer musical *Gestalt* than that provided by this movement.

Sonata in D Major (K. 311, November, 1777)

FIRST MOVEMENT (*Allegro con spirito*). This movement, in sonata form, opens with a rolled D major chord,
similar to that of the Sonata in D Major (K. 284). The
Mannheim orchestra had made a great impression upon the

young Wolfgang, so that this and the C Major Sonata (K. 309) are similar in the imitation of orchestral devices. Quite worthy of mention is the exceptional recapitulation, in which the second subject is presented before the first. This flexible conception of chronology lends an enticing patch of freshness to the composition—although it is not suggested that the work is in any sense in need of "a breath of fresh air." Far from it!

SECOND MOVEMENT *(Andante con espressione)*. The form of this movement is that of a "modified sonata." This is the nomenclature used by most writers. It has also been referred to as an "older rondo form." Percy Goetschius prefers to classify it as an "augmentation of the sonatine-form."[7]

The first theme, twelve measures in length, is gentle in its unlabored unfoldment. It reflects the lightness and happiness of the Mannheim visit. None of the somber and profound tones of the A Minor Sonata (K. 310) are found in this music.

THIRD MOVEMENT *(Rondo: Allegro)*. This section exemplifies the third rondo form, curiously extended by a modulatory episode. Fortunately, the cadenza before the recapitulation is written out, whereas quite often Mozart improvised a cadenza during the performance. The music in this last movement is full of joy and lilt in the swinging six-eight rhythm.

Sonata in A Major (K. 331, Summer, 1778)[8]

This work is aptly regarded as a creation in "Turkish" spirit. It is exceptional in that Mozart uses the theme and variations for the first movement. The D Major Sonata (K. 284) is the only other sonata employing this form.

---

[7] Percy Goetschius, *Lessons in Music Form* (1904), p. 138. For review of musical forms in general, the reader is referred to Howard A. Murphy, *Form in Music for the Listener* (1945).

[8] Discussed in Chapter Four, p. 26.

Unusual too, is the absence of the sonata form in the entire composition.

FIRST MOVEMENT *(Andante grazioso)*. A tempo of agreement should pervade the *Tema* and the first four variations. For the fifth and sixth variations the tempo is indicated by Mozart. The writer regrets to report having heard the variations played by many students and artists in varying tempos. The performer is admonished not to use this movement as a demonstration of pyrotechnics and finger facility. To do so would be to deface the very tablet of its being. Under such conditions, the interpretation is lost.[9]

SECOND MOVEMENT *(Menuetto and Trio)*. Instead of the usual *Adagio,* Mozart has used most skillfully the *Menuetto* and *Trio*. Fortunately, this music speaks for itself, and if the spirit of the eighteenth century minuet style is allowed to govern the interpretation, the reward will be satisfying.

THIRD MOVEMENT *(Alla Turca: Allegretto)*. Mozart fully intended this movement to be played with the Janissary attachment. The reader may wish to review Chapter Three, particularly page 21, before interpreting this movement.

In reality the harpsichord provides a clearer idea of the original coloring than can be achieved on the modern piano. The harpsichord has the twang of the string, to lend a nasal brilliance to the "Turkish" effect. Once the true spirit of this movement is discovered, there will be no doubt in the performer's mind about correct interpretation.

---

[9] Two observations of a tangential nature are of interest here. Tobin, describing this section, asserts: "The theme is a delightful musical moment: if correctly interpreted. The opening group of quavers should be regarded as beginning on the half-bar and swinging rhythmically up to the note E which takes the main accent. This accentuation leads to a more correct placing of the cadence chords." [Tobin, *op. cit.,* p. 88.]

Regarding the theme, Einstein comments: ". . . the theme itself is utterly French, and at the same time utterly Mozartean. Especially Mozartean is the strengthening of the end of the theme with a *forte* passage: a device that is to return with symbolic strength to Mozart's setting of Goethe's *Das Veilchen*." [Einstein, *op. cit.,* p. 245.]

Sonata in F Major (K. 332, Summer, 1778)

FIRST MOVEMENT *(Allegro)*. One might consider this section, in sonata form, one of the "popular" works of Mozart—if any work of Mozart could be so called! The opening theme consists of two sentences in the tonic key. The first is *gemütlich* in character. The establishment of a downward floating motion is effected in the second sentence; an imitation begins in measure 7. Measure 23 initiates a sudden burst of drama with climaxes on the diminished chords in measures 25–26 and 29–30. The lovely second theme is approached through its tonic minor. It is a true development built entirely on ideas from the set of second subjects. The customary recapitulation brings the first movement to its termination.

SECOND MOVEMENT *(Adagio)*. Again, the form of this movement has different interpretations, as Marks points out:

> The terms "modified sonata," "abridged sonata," and "sonatine" are variously employed by different writers to describe the form in which this movement is written, the terms being used synonymously.[10]

In view of the above, and of varying opinions of other authoritative writers, it is as well to regard this section as a "modified sonata."

The movement contains a return to the style of Johann Christian Bach. This return seems natural; Bach was in Paris early in 1778, and it is more than likely that he discussed some of his sonatas (Op. XVII), stimulating the imagination of Mozart in certain musical directions.

Hutcheson comments on the movement:

> The slow movement wears its lavish ornamentation with grace, and the additional embellishments of the early editions on the repetition of the themes, though not present in the autograph, have been adopted by pianists without hesitation.[11]

10 F. Helena Marks, *The Sonata: Its Form and Meaning* (1921), p. 80.
11 Ernest Hutcheson, *The Literature of the Piano* (1948), p. 73.

THIRD MOVEMENT *(Allegro assai).* This final movement could have been a model for some of the last movements of the Beethoven sonatas. This is Mozart in the bravura style. There is compelling rhythmic swing, coupled with brilliant thematic material to please the most discriminating audience. Hutcheson calls the work

. . . [one] of outstanding beauty, peculiarly suitable for concert performance because of its grateful pianistic quality, culminating in an exceptionally brilliant finale . . .[12]

Sonata in B Flat Major (K. 333, Summer, 1778)

FIRST MOVEMENT *(Allegro).* This movement is in sonata form. Number four of Bach's six clavier sonatas (Op. XVII) is undoubtedly the model for the first movement of this sonata.[13]

Tobin assigns this sonata to Mozart's Middle Period:

. . . with this sonata we reach the midway point in the development of Mozart, so far as the pianoforte sonatas are concerned. The evidence of this is: (1) the nature of the bridge passage, which is a continuation of the thought expressed in, and grows out of the previous matter; (2) the strong contrast of the themes: in many of the sonatas the second subject is not totally unlike the principal theme, but this sonata marks a sure advance from Haydn; (3) the middle section contains a definite thematic development; and even the bars 89–94, which form a link on dominant harmony, are suggestive of the subject matter. Undoubtedly this is one of, if not the strongest opening movements we have so far dwelt upon.[14]

With reference to the tempo of this movement, the performer is cautioned about fast playing. If the student will imagine himself a singer, and study the work from a vocal viewpoint, a much more faithful interpretation of Mozart's ideas will result.

[12] Hutcheson, *op. cit.,* p. 73.
[13] In Chapter Two of this volume, special attention was given to the influence of Johann Christian Bach upon Mozart. See pp. 9–11.
[14] Tobin, *op. cit.,* p. 100.

SECOND MOVEMENT *(Andante cantabile)*. This movement, in sonata form, is one of the high lights of Mozart's piano writing. The thematic material, as well as the harmonic accompaniment, is spontaneous, fresh, and truly Mozartean. The singing approach recommended in the study of the first movement will be of invaluable help in the interpretation of this section. The thirty-second notes, for example, in measure 4 must be performed as if sung. If the notes are played "singingly," the temptation to rush will be eliminated, and any mechanical tendencies on the part of the performer, if not eliminated (as they should be), will be minimized. Attention is called to the daring harmonic treatment of the development section at its start. It is easy to imagine the reaction of the musicians and critics of Mozart's time to such a passage!

THIRD MOVEMENT *(Allegretto grazioso)*. For once, authorities agree! This is a rondo-sonata form. It is rewarding to regard this movement in the context of a piano concerto. One might imagine the opening theme (eight measures) announced by the piano. The F major ascending scale in measure 8 is the answer of the orchestra. After eight bars, the piano is alone again. This idea is carried throughout the entire movement. Especially interesting and unusual is the cadenza (measures 164–198): composed of fragments of the principal theme, and developed in major and minor modes, it emerges in the distinct likeness of a concerto. It is the writer's conviction that Mozart must have had the piano and orchestra in mind when this monumental movement was composed. Although this study is not written in a speculative mood, the writer feels that mention of this impression may be worthy of the piano student's serious consideration for interpretation.

THE LATE PERIOD

Six years elapsed before Mozart penned another piano sonata. He was busy in Vienna with piano concertos, the piano and wind quintet, violin sonatas, quartets, and other larger forms, including the opera.

The final period opens with the C Minor Sonata, composed on October 14, 1784, and published with the C Minor Fantasia (K. 475). It was dedicated to Mozart's pupil, Thérèse von Trattner, second wife of the printer and publisher, Johann Thomas von Trattner. Since this is an outstanding work of the period, it has been selected for detailed analysis in Chapter Eight.[15] The B Flat Major Sonata (K. 570) has also been selected for a detailed account since it is, as Einstein so aptly states, "the most completely rounded of them all, the ideal of his piano sonata."[16]

The five other sonatas of the period will be briefly discussed here.

Sonata in F Major (K. 533, 1788; K. 494, 1786)

Mozart wrote the *Rondo* of this sonata (K. 494) on June 10, 1786, and the first two movements (K. 533) in January, 1788, thus forming a sonata with which he hoped to pay at least part of a debt to his publisher, Hoffmeister.

FIRST MOVEMENT *(Allegro)*. This movement, in sonata form, is remarkable for its polyphonic conception. It contains one of the longest themes in the piano sonatas. This is attributable to constant repetitions of parts in inverted form. Although Mozart did not use the fugal form in any of the sonatas, this one comes nearest to such a design because of the double counterpoint and canonic imitation which are interspersed freely and abundantly throughout the entire movement.

SECOND MOVEMENT *(Andante)*. The second movement, also in sonata form, is one of the most advanced from a

---

[15] This view can be documented amply; *e.g.*, ". . . The most important is unquestionably the celebrated one in C minor, the fire and passion of which, especially in the last movement, surpass all previous efforts, and point to what Beethoven was to achieve in the pianoforte sonata." [Otto Jahn, *The Life of Mozart* (1882), II, 459.]

[16] Einstein, *op. cit.*, p. 249.

contrapuntal and harmonic viewpoint. The development is remarkable for its inversion of parts, and especially for the dramatic progressions of thirds preceding the recapitulation. The coda utilizes fragments from the second theme.

THIRD MOVEMENT *(Rondo: Allegretto).* This *Rondo* may be considered as in either the "older" or the "modified" rondo form. Some may logically argue, too, that this movement and the two preceding movements are so unlike in style that they should still appear separately. Yet, upon closer examination, this *Rondo,* with its extraordinary *Minore* in three parts, and its *fugato* style of transition after the recapitulation, proves well worthy of the distinguished company in which it is placed.

Sonata in B Flat (K. 498a, App. 136, 1786)

This sonata is unusual for two outstanding reasons. First, it is the only sonata of Mozart's which contains four movements. Second, the authenticity of much of it is questionable. Because a closer observation of this work reveals its greatness, it deserves further study.[17]

---

[17] "In these last years, Mozart's aim, in his piano sonatas as elsewhere, was the fusion of the old and the new, the *galant* and the 'learned'; he sought constantly to give depth to *galanterie* through contrapuntal craftsmanship— but craftsmanship that remains unnoticeable. Thus I regard as an authentic work of Mozart's a sonata movement in B-flat major (K. *Anh.* 136), which the Cantor of the Thomaskirche in Leipzig, August Eberhard Müller, later silently allowed to be put forth as his own, probably because it was too late to admit or explain a partial deception or mystification of the public that had already taken place. The misunderstanding may perhaps have come about somewhat as follows: Constanze, who would have been glad to get rid of the fragmentary works of her husband, had sent one of them—the beginning of this movement—to the publisher Thonus in Leipzig for appraisal; Thonus got Müller to complete the work, and sent it out into the world under Mozart's name with the first minuet of the *Kleine Nachtmusic* (which had been lost and had somehow come into his possession) and two movements by Müller. The movement in question shows Mozart on the way to the last sonata, in D (K. 576). It is an attempt to employ both hands in the service of a texture that combines *galant* and contrapuntal elements—an attempt which, since it is not without effort and certain doctrinaire purposefulness, it is easy to understand why Mozart abandoned. But that the movement once existed, in some such form as that of the sonata movement K. 400, I have no doubt." [Einstein, *op. cit.,* p. 249.]

FIRST MOVEMENT *(Allegro moderato)*. This section, in sonata form, gives evidence of Mozart's maturity of the later period. Inversion of parts, contrapuntal passages, re-iterated staccato chords, serve not only to strengthen this concept, but also to prophesy the early Beethoven.

SECOND MOVEMENT *(Andante)*. This section is an arrangement, probably by André, of the *Andante* from the Piano Concerto in B Flat Major (K. 450, 1784). The form employed is that of theme and variations.

THIRD MOVEMENT *(Menuetto* and *Trio: Allegretto)*. In the Einstein-Köchel catalogue this *Menuetto* is considered definitely written by Mozart. Especially expert is the development in the *Menuetto* middle section.

FOURTH MOVEMENT *(Rondo: Allegro)*. This section is of irregular construction. In spite of this, it is possible to classify it as older rondo form. The writer prefers not to pass judgment as to the value of the music contained in these pages, but to suggest that the individual student examine the contents and reserve formulating definite notions until thorough study of the entire contents is accomplished.

Sonata in C Major (K. 545, June 26, 1788)

Mozart's directions indicate that this sonata was written for the neophyte. The "Little Sonata for Beginners" stands forth as a masterpiece. Some critics may pick at the weakness of its thematic content, or the lack of contrast in its design and style. But it has withstood, and will survive, the superficial insight and lamentable commentaries of those who can remain untouched by its enormously beautiful simplicity. It is a work which can be appreciated on a multiplicity of levels.[18] This "Little Sonata for Beginners," from

---

[18] To paraphrase the words of Victor Balaguer, attempting to put into words his feelings about the immortal story of *Don Quixote,* "As a boy I [heard] it, and laughed, but as a man I again [heard] it, and wept." Such is the wide range of emotional appeal in this "Little Sonata for Beginners." A keynote of greatness is simplicity.

the interpretive viewpoint, paradoxically tests the powers of the maturest artist—not to mention the beginner!

The writer feels that although this sonata may fall within the technical grasp of the uninitiated, and may be played (as it usually is, unfortunately) without a mature concept of color and intensity of interpretation, it is truly a Mozartean masterpiece clothed in inimitable simplicity.

FIRST MOVEMENT *(Allegro)*. This section, in perfect sonata form (considering the use of free fantasia for the development section, rather than a "working out" of thematic materials) should be played with bell-like clarity. Any attempt to make technical brilliance an end in itself rather than a means to achieve the interpretive goal, would be to violate the spirit of the work.

SECOND MOVEMENT *(Andante)*. This section, although it gives the impression of being a rondo, is in ternary form. Unless the thematic material is colored with exquisite taste, monotony may rob the movement of its simple, straightforward, and highly spiritual message.

THIRD MOVEMENT *(Rondo: Allegretto grazioso)*. This *Rondo* is of the older form. It is especially interesting for the opening passage, which is conceived in strict imitation with a canon in the fifth below. Here again, the lack of contrast in the episodes calls for imagination in interpreting these two pages; otherwise a certain dullness will inevitably prevail. This necessitates the resourcefulness of maturity in interpretation.

Sonata in F Major (K. 547a)

This unusual sonata, according to several accounts, may not be Mozart's work.[19]

19 Marks: "Neither this sonata nor the following one in B flat major [K. 498a or App. III, 136] is included in the chronological portion of Köchel's Catalogue [K. 498a is Einstein's revision, 1937, after Marks' book was published], but they are placed in the third appendix. The reason for this is that neither of the two sonatas is original in the form here presented. . . . The opening Allegro of this sonata, for instance, is an arrangement of a

FIRST MOVEMENT *(Allegro)*. Sonata form characterizes this "arrangement." While the work may not reflect the
master Mozart as do the other sonatas, it is worth studying,
and, in the writer's opinion, would make an excellent teaching piece for an intermediate student, since it possesses no
real technical, harmonic, or interpretive problems that cannot be solved by the average pupil.

SECOND MOVEMENT *(Allegretto)*. This section is a
transposition of the third movement of the Sonata in C
Major (K. 545); and the comments on that movement,
given earlier in this chapter, apply here. Einstein believes
it is definitely by Mozart because the coda is an improvement
over that of the original version in the earlier sonata.

Sonata in D Major (K. 576, 1789)

This is the last sonata in the late period. It is definitely
in the same category as the great C Minor Sonata (K. 457),
although it may not possess the drama of the earlier work.
Even if it lacks some of the greater emotional depth, it is
Mozart at his zenith from a purely pianistic point of view.

It was written as one of the six "easy" sonatas.[20] One has
but to traverse the first few pages to discover that the word
"easy" is a misnomer. The writer considers this to be the
most difficult of all the sonatas from a technical standpoint.
It is rich in counterpoint reminiscent of Johann Sebastian
Bach.[21]

FIRST MOVEMENT *(Allegro)*. This movement, in sonata

movement from a sonata for piano and violin (Köchel No. 547) whilst the
Rondo is also an arrangement—or, more strictly speaking, it is virtually a
transposition—of the finale of the easy Sonata in C major, for pianoforte
alone, No. 16, in this volume (Köchel No. 545). Both the original works are
dated June 26, 1788, but when, and by whom, these adaptions were made is
unknown." [Marks, *op. cit.*, p. 155.]

Tobin: "The Zimmermann edition declares that the date of composition of
this sonata is unknown. The first movement is curiously unequal. The opening theme leads to nowhere." [Tobin, *op. cit.*, p. 129.]

[20] According to a letter from Mozart to Puchberg, July 12–14, 1789. [Emily
Anderson, *Letters of Mozart and His Family* (1938), III, 1384.]

[21] J. S. Bach's influence upon Mozart is discussed on pages 14–17.

form, begins with a typical "hunting" motive. The idea is entirely new in the piano sonatas, and forms a rhythmic phrase around which Mozart weaves his polyphonic patterns. The performer would do well to emphasize the "hunting" motive in the bass passage (measure 8 with upbeat to measure 15). Even here, the arpeggios (measures 15–18) and the typical "horn" intervals (measures 19–25) may be brought out to advantage.

SECOND MOVEMENT *(Adagio)*. Percy Goetschius calls this movement "first rondo-form."[22] This is one of the most exquisite of the Mozartean slow movements. If the florid passages are played with a coloratura vocal line in mind, the temptation to hasten, or to emphasize the technical aspects, will be overcome.

THIRD MOVEMENT *(Allegretto)*. The consensus is that this movement is in irregular sonata form. Since there is very little contrast between the first and second themes in either rhythm or melodic line, this presents a severe test to the interpreter to add emotional zest so that interest may not wane. Unless technical perfection has been attained, the left-hand passages in measures 9–12 and 46–48 will prove a trammel for the performer.

[22] Goetschius, *op. cit.*, p. 110.

Eight

SELECTED SONATAS:
AN ANALYSIS

THE EARLY PERIOD

Sonata in G Major (K. 283, Winter, 1774)

This sonata is the best-known of the Early Period. It is indeed one of the most alluring and graceful in the eighteenth century piano literature. Responsible observers disagree concerning the musical value of this work, but it continues to draw the enduring interest of amateur as well as professional performers. The writer votes with those who believe in this work's value.

FIRST MOVEMENT *(Allegro)*. The form of the first movement is a subject of debate. It possesses the contours of a sonatina. Marks and Tobin agree that it is sonata form. The former contends:

In this movement a short episode which bears slightly, but only slightly, upon the exposition, takes the place of the customary working out section.[1]

Referring to the above-cited episode, Hadow substantiates this view:

[1] F. Helena Marks, *The Sonata: Its Form and Meaning* (1921), p. 28.

They belong exclusively to the earlier period of the free fantasia. . . . Even where they occur—e.g., in Mozart's Sonata in G (No. 5) the episode generally bears some sort of relation to the Exposition —i.e., it is not a new idea altogether, but one which bears resemblances, however remote, to the phraseology of the first or second subject.[2]

Exposition—First Theme: It is interesting to note that the quarter rests on the second beat of the opening bars (1–4) are as vital to the theme as the notes constituting the melodic line. In view of this, the performer is admonished to use the damper pedal sparingly. Perhaps Mozart had in mind a dialogue—question and answer, metaphorically speaking—between the soprano and the alto.

Expansion: The upbeat to measure 5 is the first of three attempts of the melodic line to expand. The performer must not be misled by the *forte-piano* indications in measures 5 and 6. These indications are Mozart's prescriptions and must be followed with a degree of faithfulness; yet the passage will be more enhanced by increased sonority on each successive upbeat leading to the *forte-piano,* than by complete reliance on this dynamic indication alone. The teacher or student performing Mozart with this sort of approach to the three upbeats will give added direction to the movement, culminating in an escape to the scale passage in measure 8.

Bridge to Second Theme: The bridge to the second theme is another instance of three attempts to expand, with the final attempt succeeding in measure 18. This could be treated interpretively in the same manner as above.

Second Theme: If the moving line in the left hand of measures 23 and 24 is brought out slightly, the syncopated rhythmic element will aid in the projection of the second theme. The performer will note that this theme is intensified by the use of sixteenth notes in both hands in measures 27 to 30. Strict observance of the *staccato* and *legato, forte*

and *piano* indications in measures 30 to 33 will be rewarding, interpretively. The recalling of the "three attempts"
mentioned previously will aid again in shaping the orientation of the music.

The ornament in measures 43–44 should start on the
upper auxiliary and may consist of three notes in the right
hand against two in the left. This produces a quick, yet
clear, embellishment:

[Written]   [Played]

If the right hand is accentuated *slightly* on the offbeat of
the syncopated passage (measures 45–46) rather than on
the beat in measures 48–49, the intensity will rise steadily
to the cadence of the exposition.

Episode: It is essential that the appoggiatura in measure
53 (as well as in the measures that follow) be played *on*
the beat, and not before (see Chapter Five). Again, the
warning: *do not use* the damper pedal. The only exception
would be a touch at the beginning of measures 61, 63, and
65.

Recapitulation: A slight retard in measure 70 will prepare the way for the return of the first theme, which is
modified in measure 74. The element of surprise in the
forte thirds in the left hand leading into A minor confirms
the genius of Mozart for invention. Thus, the repetition
with the exception of the key of the same material as was
heard in the exposition brings this movement to a close.

SECOND MOVEMENT *(Andante).* The design of the
second movement is sonata form. Tobin and Marks main-

tain that the first theme is, in reality, an eight-bar sentence, and that the movement should have been written in two-four instead of four-four time. Tobin clarifies this:

"Such errors are of frequent occurrence in the works of great masters." Prout [author of *Musical Form,* London: Augener] says this simply arises from inattention on the part of composers who are often in-different, so long as the cadence comes on an accent, whether that accent is strong or weak.[3]

Exposition—First Theme: In the opening bar of the theme, the repeated C should be played so as to prolong the sound, rather than to gain in intensity. The simplicity of such utterance will be far superior if approached from this viewpoint. Quite daring and unawaited is the decrescendo beginning with measure 7; for usually an ascending line demands an increase in tonal volume.

Second Theme: This phrase commences in the dominant (measure 9). Marks' interpretive note is:

The special point to notice in this subject is in the responsive phrase (11–14) and arises from the fact that the movement is barred, as above mentioned, in four-quarter instead of in two-quarter time. The passage . . . written as bars 11–12 is immediately repeated *overlapping* from bar 12–14, and thus apparently causes *inversion of the accents.* That the inversion is only apparent and not real will be conclusively proved by re-writing the movement in two-quarter time, when the first notes, both of the original phrase and of its repetition, *will fall on the strong accent of the bar.*[4]

Mozart startles his listener with an approach just the op-posite to the decrescendo in measures 7 and 8. The inten-sity in the last quarter of measure 15 has been cited in a con-sideration of harmonies and tonalities (Chapter Four).

Development: The nine bars of development deal chiefly with the first theme in the keys of D minor, C major, and A minor, after which an ascending chromatic passage leads into the recapitulation.

[3] J. Raymond Tobin, *Mozart and the Sonata Form* (1916), p. 54.
[4] Marks, *op. cit.,* p. 29.

Recapitulation: The first theme is modified in measure 28, forming a dominant seventh in F major. The transition in this new key leads through a modulation to C major to a final statement of the second theme.

Coda: A short coda is based upon the first theme, yet situated in a new harmonic habitat. Banister has eloquently remarked upon this coda: "It takes a last fond look at the subject."[5]

THIRD MOVEMENT *(Presto).*   The form of the movement is sonata form.

Exposition—First Theme: This movement might easily be mistaken for a rondo, with its joyous theme of eight bars rippling over a pedal point. Yet this concept is modified when the development and recapitulation appear.

The performer should not play this movement too hurriedly, even though it is marked *Presto.* A metronome mark of 92–96 to the dotted quarter will give an indication of the speed at which the movement retains its vigor without loss of clarity.

Second Theme: In measure 41, the second theme is announced in a gentle manner. The pedal point on the A in measures 43–45 can still be retained if a slight pressure is exerted on this note in measures 46–47. The effect is that of an echo—unforgettably beautiful in this and similar passages. The chord on the third beat of measures 65–68 will be more vital and rhythmic if played entirely by the left hand, rather than as indicated.

Development: Measure 103 in D minor initiates one of the most dramatic developments in Mozart's early works. The diminished chord in measure 107 with the descending broken thirds leading to A minor in measure 111, and the ensuing similar passages reveal Mozart's power of intensity and feeling and illustrate his use of the diminished chord as explained in Chapter Four.

[5] Henry C. Banister, *Lectures on Musical Analysis* (1902), p. 276.

The chromatic run in measures 168–169 ends the development section abruptly, whereupon a measure rest leads to the conclusion.

Recapitulation: Here Mozart's adherence to accepted form is precise. The movement ends with the usual V₇-I, and is augmented by a measure rest before and after the final chord.

Sonata in D Major (K. 284, March, 1775)

Among the piano sonatas, this is one of the most unusual of Mozart's conceptions. He composed it for Baron Thaddäus von Dürnitz, who apparently provided indications for many of the ideas found in the fabric of the work. It is clearly orchestral in feeling. This is particularly the case with the first movement. Furthermore, it is a blend of "French" and "Italian" styles. The sonata is brilliant beyond anything Mozart had composed to this point.

FIRST MOVEMENT *(Allegro).* The first movement is written in sonata form. Whether the performer wishes to treat the middle section as a free fantasy or as a development is relatively unimportant. The point is controversial and its significance within the over-all perspective does not justify consideration here.

Exposition—First Theme: The first subject is announced with a rolled chord. The roll is, undoubtedly, a vestige from the harpsichord style. The quarter rest, following the chord, enables the performer to time the gesture necessary to return to the keyboard after the initial raising of the hand on the chord. The appoggiaturas on the third and fourth quarters of the measure are to be played as sixteenth notes. These should be accentuated, thus highlighting the dissonance. While the three quarter notes in unison in the second measure are to be completely separated, the ensuing eighth notes are merely detached (since Mozart has omitted the *legato* phrase line). Observance of the *piano* and *forte* markings in measures 4–7 will produce the desired orchestral effect. During this entire exposition, the effect of brilliancy which Mozart apparently intended should be sustained. Measures 13–21 must be maintained *forte* and relentlessly intense to the final bar.

Second Theme: This theme, commencing in measure 22, is lyrical in nature, and forms a contrast to the majestic opening subject. Eighteenth century phrasing (ever so slight a pause, more mental than physical, after the chord resolutions and cadences) will dictate a new start on the passage (third quarter of measure 25), not on the A (first sixteenth), but on the B (second sixteenth). The A is a resolution to the tonic harmonies in the first half of this measure.

If the performer will accent slightly the first and third beats in the left hand of measures 28–29, the syncopation in the right hand will be vitalized and the rhythm thus enhanced. Measure 33 is climactic in the intensity of this section. One must keep in mind two distinct voices of the right hand in the second half of measure 34 and the entire measure 35. Measure 39 leads directly into the *forte* of measure 40; any break between the two would cause this passage to become meaningless. The exposition ends with what Fisher terms a "codetta" (measures 50–51).[6]

Development: Marks refers to this section as an "episode,"[7] whereas Tobin employs the term "development."[8] For present purposes, the latter term is perfectly adequate.

The development section is teeming with inversion of parts and sequential designs. The opening measure 52, in A minor, commences a series of question-and-answer patterns. The left hand leads in each case, conducting an exquisite melodic interview with the right. Although Mozart has failed to indicate the dynamics of the first eight bars,

[6] Henry Fisher, *The Musical Examinee* (1845), p. 143.

[7] "The second part of this movement consists wholly of an episode. Although, in the usual acceptation of the term, there is no *development* of material from the first part, the *germ* of the episode is to be found there." [Marks, *op. cit.*, p. 35.]

[8] Tobin, *op. cit.*, p. 59.

the performer would be following good taste to play measures 52–53 *forte,* measures 54–55 *piano,* and continue this volume design until the dynamic indications begin in measure 60. Such an effect, while appearing "black and white," metaphorically speaking, will alleviate the obvious sequential mosaic in this section. Mozart uses the more remote keys of A minor, E minor, B minor, F sharp minor, to render this passage dramatically intense. Observe that the dynamics for both right and left hand in measures 60–68 are unmistakably indicated and should be followed. The diminished seventh chord, on the second beat in measure 64, seems to be the emotional climax of the development. The scale fragments in measures 70–71 lead into the recapitulation.

Recapitulation: With the exception of the extension of the "ladder" passage[9] in measures 97–98, and the material forming an extension from measure 119 to the codetta (ritornello), the recapitulation adheres to the usual form and is to be interpreted in the manner of the exposition.[10]

SECOND MOVEMENT *(Rondeau en Polonaise: Andante).* It is uncommon in Mozart to find the slow movement of a sonata written in rondo form; and this movement is doubly unusual in having the dance pattern of a polonaise.[11]

Principal Theme: This is an eight-measure sentence in A major, repeated and varied. Dynamics in various editions are inconsistent. The Urtext (Kalmus edition), generally considered the most faithful to the original, errs, I believe, in this passage; however, musical discretion will caution the performer to be consistent in following the dynamic indications of whatever edition he employs. The

---

[9] Ascending broken thirds.

[10] Tobin says: "The conclusion of the recapitulation differs from that of the exposition. It is . . . doubtful if any portion could be regarded as coda; for the new matter is in the nature of an interpolation (bar 119) rather than an addition." [Tobin, *op. cit.,* p. 59.]

[11] Niecks defines: "Polonaise (Fr.)—a chivalrous Polish dance in three-quarter time and of dignified but animated movement." [F. Niecks, *Dictionary of Musical Terms* (1884), p. 194.]

Breitkopf and Härtel edition gives what the writer considers the correct dynamics: the mark is not simply *f*, but *fz*—followed by *p* on the second beat. The *fz* is to be played with stress or additional accent.[12]

Episode: An episode consisting of two free variations is introduced in the tonic in measure 17. In this and the following two bars, there is no surcease from the rhythmic drive of the polonaise.

Mozart has ingeniously reversed the dynamics in the return of the principal theme (measure 31). Strangely, however, with this violent contrast, the polonaise rhythm remains untouched.

In the transition to the second episode, introduced by measure 47, there are three measures of repeated C sharps in the upper voice. The intensity will be sharpened if these repeated notes are treated in a cumulative fashion leading to the climax on the first beat of the following measure.

Return to Principal Theme: The final return of the principal theme is intensified by the Alberti bass in the left hand and the use of a thirty-second note trill with ornamental termination on the last beat of measures 71–73. The cadential repetitions give the impression of a coda, bringing the second movement to a close.

THIRD MOVEMENT *(Andante)*. The most unique feature of this sonata is the *Tema* and twelve variations constituting the last movement. Mozart also utilized the variation form for the first movement of the Sonata in A Major (K. 331).

Theme: The *Tema* is considered as a ternary or three-part idea.[13] The Urtext (Kalmus edition) fails to record the tempo marking of *Andante*—definitely Mozart's direction—which appears in the very old Breitkopf and Härtel edition. The *Tema* and the first six variations should be

---

[12] See Niecks, *op. cit.*, p. 217.
[13] Stewart Macphereson, *Form in Music* (1930), pp. 87–88.

played in the same tempo. The tempo may be slightly slower in the *Minore* Variation VII, although Mozart has given no directions for it. A return to the original tempo in the *Maggiore* Variation VIII, and in Variations IX and X, is imperative for a contrasting statement of the *Adagio cantabile* Variation XI. For the last variation (XII), Mozart has indicated *Allegro*.

Variations: Einstein sums up the exceptional nature of the variations thus:

> Particularly remarkable is the sonority and the unity of the variations. Mozart had written out piano variations in the preceding years; those on an arietta by Saliere (K. 180) in 1773, and the so-called Fischer Variations (K. 179) in 1774, which he used for a long time as a virtuoso display piece. But they are merely charming or brilliant in comparison to the rich flow of invention in these later variations, in which there is included, for the first time, the *minore,* a variation in minor lending its chromaticism to the variety of the whole. Not even the somewhat old-fashioned and lengthy adagio variation interrupts the flow of the creative imagination.[14]

Variation I. The first variation, using triplets in the treble, has an eighteenth century type of phrase marking in most editions. The first two measures, seemingly phrased in sixes, should be carried over to the seventh tone, which is on the beat. The third full measure has the slur over each triplet figure. Complete adherence to this phrasing is necessary for the rhythmic as well as the thematic interpretation. The performer is cautioned not to hasten this variation.

Variation II. The question-and-answer pattern is the chief characteristic of this portion. The variation's effectiveness is contingent upon a clear, simple delineation of the basic pattern.

Variation III. The tempo of Variation III should be used as a guide for the movement of all variations except the *Minore* (VII) and those individually marked (XI and

---

14 Alfred Einstein, *Mozart—His Character, His Work* (1945), p. 243.

XII). Variations III and IV are the most difficult technically, and should be played fast enough to cause the *Tema* to have a sense of destiny and direction. Yet, a *presto* tempo is not consistent with the spirit of this variation. Technique, in this movement particularly, must be relegated to the secondary and kept as unobtrusive as possible.

Variation IV. The opening quarter note A in the bass of this unusual variation must be played as part of the thematic. context. It belongs to the upbeat of the first phrase. The *staccato* marking on the note is intended to give it a punctuating *pizzicato* effect, upon the conclusion of which a new motion in the melodic line is initiated.

Variation V. While Variations III and IV project a bravura quality in the *forte* vein, this section, in contrast, should be interpreted tranquilly and with restraint. Crucial to the spirit of this variation, the thirds in the bass passages must be performed with a maximum of *legato*.

Variation VI. This is a return to the bravura style. The descending octave figure commencing this variation should be given a sober, even majestic, quality. In a sense, it is ponderous. Each succeeding appearance of this figure during the variation should be treated similarly. The question-and-answer design, so characteristic of Mozart, reappears here. The inquiring, conversational spirit permeates the melodic line, making for a kind of *Wahlverwandtschaft* (elective affinity) between the right hand and the left. The performer should play this section with a constant awareness of the congenial possibilities Mozart gave to it.

Variation VII *(Minore)*. This is one of the loveliest of the variations, and is not without unique facets as a *minore* statement. It is a refreshing respite in the minor—like an oasis in a desert of major sounds. A quiet, serious quality should pervade the traversal of this short but tonally luminous moment.

Variation VIII *(Maggiore)*. With the introduction of octaves in the treble, this variation returns to the regal style of writing. In orchestral metaphor, the octaves are flowing but strident spokesmen for the brasses. A contrast with Variation VII should be remarked by the performer, but should not be made too obvious.

Variation IX. This section is in a contrapuntal vein. The canonic treatment initiated in measure 4 is singular and offers exciting possibilities for the performer who is sensitized to the largeness of Mozart's contrapuntal idea.

Variation X. The orchestral medium again asserts itself in this variation. The performer should imagine an effect of tremolo strings in suspension around a horn passage enunciating the bass. The second half of measure 4 reverses this procedure, with the broken octaves in the bass and the syncopated wood winds in the treble. This alternating effect is sharply pointed up if an ever-accumulating energy is directed properly from the opening to the conclusion.

Variation XI (Adagio cantabile). This is one of the most endearing of Mozart's piano works, in the writer's judgment. The variation calls for imaginative interpretation. It is less orchestral than operatic in character, and should be played as a soprano aria: the fingers must sing the melodic message. A successful effort in this direction will at once make manifest Mozart's splendid conception. The Urtext (Kalmus edition) gives the ornamentation as indicated in the autograph and also as indicated in Toricella's edition. The Toricella, published in Vienna in 1784, was the first edition; Mozart always preferred it. It shows how Mozart intended the manuscripts to be played, and, as usual, the manuscript is a kind of shorthand version which the composer elaborated in detail upon its publication. We can be sure the Toricella is true Mozart.

Variation XII (Allegro). This, the last of the variations, opens in the style of a minuet. But the style continues for only five measures, giving way to a bravura expression in measures 9–16, where the intensification of the bass achieves the transition. This treatment is reminiscent of the first movement. Special assertiveness must be reserved for the broadening in the penultimate measure. Thus ends a sonata which richly exemplifies Mozart's wealth of musical ingenuity and good taste.

Two other works notable for this ingenuity and taste are the two sonatas in C major (K. 309 and K. 330), from the Middle Period. These are analyzed in the following pages.

THE MIDDLE PERIOD

Sonata in C Major (K. 309, November 8, 1777)

From Augsburg, in a letter of October 23–24, 1777, Mozart wrote to his father:

My concert duly took place yesterday, Wednesday, the 22nd . . . then all of a sudden a magnificent Sonata in C Major, out of my head, and a Rondo to finish up with. There was a regular din of applause.[15]

With this account from Mozart's hand, we are definitely informed about the birth of this composition.

FIRST MOVEMENT *(Allegro con spirito)*. Sonata form of the early type is used in this movement. By this is meant the use of free fantasia for the development. The second theme does not appear in the working-out section.

Exposition—First Theme: The first theme, of eight bars' length, has the character of a transcription of a symphony for the piano. The unison opening is particularly orchestral in quality. It is evident from the arpeggiated harmony on the opening beat that Mozart intended the octave C to dominate the chord formed by this device. The arpeggiated tones must start *on* the beat, like a very short ornament— forming a rolled chord, typical of opening movements of that time.

A slight pressure on the C sharp in the bass (third quarter

[15] Emily Anderson, *Letters of Mozart and His Family* (1938), II, 493, and 498.

of measure 3) and on the B (third quarter of measure 4) will accentuate both the melodic and the rhythmic content of these bars.

Mozart has indicated *sforzato (sf)* for the diminished chords in measures 13 and 14. That Mozart was aware of the dramatic power of chords is shown in Chapter Four. The *sforzato* is used here to increase the intensity of the approach to the octave C's in the treble (measure 15).

Second Theme: The bass introducing the second theme commencing in measure 33 is similar to the bass preceding the second theme in the C Major Sonata K. 545. The theme is repeated without change until the last half of measure 42. Measure 45 is interesting as an example of Mozart's use of diminution.[16]

In order to preserve a climactic unity, one should have a goal in view. The dramatic diminished chord in measure 50 is perhaps the highest point of intensity before the closing of the exposition. Measures 54–58 form a codetta.

Development: That Mozart selected the key of G minor for the opening of the movement is not an accident. This key was remote in its relation to C major.[17] Since the key of C major in itself does not express dramatic power, the contrast of G minor used in relation with C major is emotionally telling. The key of D minor, with its stormy qualities, and A minor, used by Mozart as a tragic key, are also utilized in this dramatic unfoldment.

Recapitulation: The first theme returns extended and modified. Especially worth noting is the employment of the theme in the tonic minor, after it has been stated in the major, at the start of the reprise. This was a daring procedure. With the exception of the inversion of parts (measures 129–132) there is but slight alteration in the second theme.

---

[16] "Diminution" means the compressing of a theme into notes of shorter duration, while keeping the melodic material the same.

[17] See Chapter Four.

Since the ritornello is the same as in the exposition, the coda begins at the fourth measure from the end of the movement.[18]

SECOND MOVEMENT *(Andante un poco adagio).* The movement is in song form, with the parts varied on repetition. Of this movement Mozart wrote:

> The Andante will give us the most trouble, for it is full of expression and must be played accurately and with the exact shades of forte and piano, precisely as they are marked.[19]

Mozart spoke enthusiastically of this movement as a character portrait of Mlle. Cannabich:

> Yesterday she again gave me indescribable pleasure; she played the whole of my sonata—excellently. The Andante *(which must not be taken too quickly)* she plays with the utmost expression. Moreover she likes playing it. I had already finished the Allegro, as you know, on the day after my arrival, and thus had only seen Mlle. Cannabich once. Young Danner asked me how I thought of composing the Andante. I said that I would make it fit closely the character of Mlle. Rosa. When I played it, it was an extraordinary success. Young Danner told me so afterwards. It really is a fact. She is exactly like the Andante.[20]

There is some confusion regarding this "portrait." Some interpreters feel that the *Andante con espressione* from the Sonata in D Major (K. 311) is the portrait that Mozart mentions.[21]

First Theme: The complete theme is sixteen measures in length. The broken syncopated thirds in F major announce

18 Mozart wrote to his father in a letter from Mannheim (November 14–16, 1777): "I shall have the sonata which I have written for Mlle. Cannabich copied out on small paper and shall send it to my sister. I began to teach it to Mlle. Rosa three days ago. *We finished the opening Allegro today.*" [Anderson, *op. cit.,* II, 548. Italics mine.]

19 *Ibid.,* II, 549.

20 *Ibid.,* II, 602.

21 Excerpts from letters are presented here in order that the student of Mozart may strive to interpret the music in terms of the background of its creation, which is helpful in reconstructing the sonatas in their broadest design. The "portrait" in itself is not the crucial factor, but merely a means to further understanding.

this tender motive. One notices, as in the Sonata in G Major (K. 283), three attempts of the ascending motive to reach its climax (see page 62). This height is finally achieved in the second quarter of measure 3, and it is maintained through the cadence in the first half of the following measure.

Second Theme: The second theme begins in measure 33. It is accompanied by repeated thirds in the bass. Such treatment lends movement to the thematic material.

In this ingenious movement, Mozart has embellished both themes with passage work and ornaments until the simplicity of the original is almost forgotten.

Coda: Cadential repetitions form a short coda.

THIRD MOVEMENT *(Rondo: Allegretto grazioso).* Instead of the usual rondo, Mozart has strayed from the proverbial straight and narrow path after the central episode in F major. Tobin offers a concise account of this "strange" procedure:

A departure from the accepted plan should be noted in that the third part opens with the *second* subject. One can imagine that in the early days of the use of the rondo-sonata form such employment of the second theme served to emphasize its presence in the scheme of things. Perhaps, too, Mozart felt that a complete résumé of the first part would have dwarfed the middle part. The restatement of the first subject would have satisfied; but might only have increased the lack of proportion. The presentation of the second theme and a conclusion with the main theme was a happy solution of a real difficulty.[22]

First Theme: The first theme of 16 measures is elongated by cadential repetitions. In this manner, three more bars are added. Typical Mozartean lilt characterizes this joyous melody. The tonality of C major is amply emphasized in the transition beginning with measure 19 and carrying through measure 38.

22 Tobin, *op. cit.,* p. 64.

Second Theme: This phrase of descending triplets (every other one drops an interval of a third) was used often by Mozart, especially in the later sonatas. The second theme of the first movement of the F Major Sonata (K. 533) is built upon this principle. Also, the developmental section of the slow movement *(Andante)* of the same sonata utilizes this figure. Again in measure 9 of the last movement *(Allegretto)* of the D Major Sonata (K. 576) the same pattern is implemented.

Admirable is the *piano* echo in measures 43 and 47. This has an added effectiveness because Mozart lowered the E natural in measure 42 to E flat in measure 43. The treble *fortissimo* tremolo in orchestral style (measures 58–61) serves as an inverted pedal over the "horn" passage in the bass. New material, episodic and thematic, is interspersed between these themes.

Codetta: A codetta, using the principal theme, brings the movement to a close—not in the brilliant manner, but quite the contrary—in a striking *pianissimo* finale.

Sonata in C Major (K. 330)

Since it was through the study and performance of this sonata that the writer's work with the piano music of Mozart became a special devotion, it will be understandable if real affection is apparent in the analysis to come. The conciseness of the musical language, the beauty of the simple thematic content, and the purity of the harmonic structuring of this work inspired the writer to probe deeper into Mozart's life and music.

FIRST MOVEMENT *(Allegro moderato)*. The first movement is in sonata form.

Exposition—First Theme: This theme is twelve bars long, announced by a lively motive in measures 1 and 2. There is an exact repetition in measures 3 and 4, with only one exception: the first of the two eighth notes in the treble is divided into two sixteenths. One would be led to believe, upon superficial examination, that this change is of little importance. Yet deeper study will reveal that this seemingly minor alteration is a device which Mozart frequently employs for the purpose of intensification. The first note of the broken octave in measure 7 must be played *on* the beat, and the trill in this same bar begins on the auxiliary. Instead of the accustomed resolution of the trill, Mozart has delayed it by inserting the lower auxiliary on the first beat of measure 8. This momentary dissonance is another contrivance in Mozart's writing which not only avoids the effect of inanity in the cadence but creates a feeling of movement which completes the musical idea. Measures 5 and 6 are repeated in measures 9 and 10, but the addition of thirty-second notes in the ascending broken chords of the soprano produces the necessary intensification for compelling interest.

Second Theme: The second theme opens in measure 19 with a short appoggiatura played *on* the beat. The second half of this measure is an exact repetition of the first half. The full writing out of the treble C sharp and D as sixteenth notes in the second half of this measure, instead of the appoggiatura as previously employed, yields a significant clue to the interpretation. Mozart used the short appoggiatura in the first half of the measure, thus enabling the two sixteenths to emphasize the dissonance in repetition.

To the interpreter who is not emotionally immersed in Mozart, this aspect of the analysis may seem unnecessary. But the fullest meaning of the passages just cited cannot possibly be revealed unless these minor details are rigorously observed. Fortunately, Mozart is consistent in his style; so an understanding of an interpretive detail in the passage quoted will facilitate the reading of similar passages in other works of Mozart.

The three-bar phrase in measures 29–31, with a climax on the *sforzato* diminished chord in the last measure, furnishes a relief from the somewhat self-repetitive two-bar rhythm.

The second part of the second theme begins on the *sforzato* (measure 34) and continues until measure 42, where the third part commences. A short coda (measures 54–58) brings the exposition to a close.

Development: Since there is no real "working out" of the subject matter, there is controversy as to the structural nomenclature for this section. In the strictest sense of the term, it is not a "development." It consists principally of a free fantasia which utilizes fresh passages remotely evocatory of the first subject.

Special attention is invited to the echo or repetition in measure 63. A glorious effect will be achieved if this measure, with its *sforzatos* on the E flats, is played *pianissimo*. An ever-so-slight holding of these E flats will further emphasize the tenderness of this passage.

The "three attempts," or thematic allusions, will be found in measures 66–68. Measures 69–70 form the climax as the motive matures. Measure 88 announces the recapitulation.

Recapitulation: The second theme's return in the original key of G major is unusually striking. In strict form, this theme should return in the tonic (i.e., C major). At this point, the student of Mozart's works realizes that much of the genius manifested in his creations comes from subtle attempts to defy man-made laws and strict forms. Mozart continues the return of the second theme in the key of G major until measure 109. Then, with a touch of rare intuition (as if this were ever absent in Mozart!), he introduces an F natural as the first bass note of this same measure, and on it builds up the third inversion of the dominant seventh in the key of C major. As a consequence, the second theme is restated in the correct key at measure 110.

Coda: In this segment of the work, beginning at measure 145, there are fragments from the opening of the development (free-fantasia) section. These motives are supported by the tonic pedal (i.e., C major). If a slight emphasis is given to the note F in the bass from measure 148 to the *sforzato* chord in the final bar, a very tasteful harmonic effect will be realized. The F will naturally resolve to the E in the final chord.

SECOND MOVEMENT *(Andante cantabile)*. Authorities disagree as to the form of this movement. Some call it ternary or three-part form, while others refer to it as episodical. The writer feels that "three-part form" more precisely describes the structure. Tobin, considering the movement's form, was moved to say:

After listening to these two pages of sheer music one would be disinclined to question or examine the structural plan did not the words of Robert Schumann come to mind: "Only when the form becomes clear to you will the spirit become so too." Examine then the plan of the movement, and play it over again and again until the understanding is perfect; for this is a movement which we will never outgrow.[23]

Principal Theme: The beauty of this motive lies in its utter simplicity. The three C's forming the upbeat to the first measure must grow in intensity. Here, the decision as to exactly how much to intensify will depend entirely upon the good judgment and taste of the performer. In such a simple utterance, it would be disastrous to exaggerate the crescendo in this figure.

If the passage from the initial bar to the third quarter of measure 4 is felt and played as one phrase, the unity of melodic design will be greatly strengthened and preserved.

The middle section in F minor, beginning at measure 21, is unforgettable. Mozart has used the identical three-note upbeat to this section as in the beginning of the movement, with the exception that it is presented in sixths instead of single notes. In an orchestral arrangement, the repeated

[23] Tobin, *op. cit.*, p. 83.

notes in the bass would undoubtedly be played by the bassoon. The lovely section which follows, opening with two measures in A flat major, is neatly contrapuntal in its workmanship. Then the first part of the middle section returns; and the E natural in the treble of the last measure is unusual in the effect it gives within the context. After the principal theme is restated, there is a short coda founded upon the motive of the second theme. This coda is in the major.

Thus, Mozart has given to humanity a moment of perfection, understandable only to those whose hearts have been opened to the greatness of such simplicity.

THIRD MOVEMENT *(Allegretto)*.   The movement is in sonata form.

Exposition—First Theme: The first theme, sixteen-bars long, light in quality, reminds one of the entrance of the solo piano part of a concerto. The orchestra reiterates the opening motive (measures 9–14) and the piano joins the orchestra in measure 15, carrying the dominant role through measure 20. The piano plays in triplets in the treble, while the orchestra supplies the harmonic accompaniment in the bass chords. The intensity is also heightened in measures 9–14 by the surging arpeggios interspersed with broken octaves played by the left hand.

Once again, the student is cautioned about the temptation to play this movement faster than the original marking *(Allegretto)* dictates. The triplet figure (measures 16–19) has a tendency to cause acceleration without the performer's realizing as much. Any undue haste will destroy the interpretive qualities revealed only by correct tempo.

An episode in measures 21–32 presents new and interesting material which might easily be mistaken for the second theme, except for the fact that it is in the tonic.

Second Theme: The second theme opens in measure 33 with a broken octave in the treble. Mozart evidently liked the accompanying figure in the bass: it is continued for a bar and a half after the treble of the first phrase has ceased. The ornaments in measures 39–41 and measures 43–45 must begin on the auxiliary, and may consist of a turn as a substitution for the trill. The second section of the theme beginning in measure 47 continues until the entrance of the coda (measure 61).

Development: The full flowering of the free fantasia emerges at measure 69 (the double bar) in the fashion of a simple songlike episode. There is no actual development, or "working out," of the previous thematic material. The first half of the new motive is repeated with a modified form of the Alberti bass in the left hand, beginning a retransition to the restatement. Measures 81–84 are formed by sequential patterns of measures 79–80. After a brief moment in the key of C minor, alternating between the tonic and the dominant, the principal theme returns in measure 96.

Recapitulation: With the exception of modification of the transition in measures 124–129 and the return of the second theme in the tonic, the recapitulation is unaltered from the exposition.

Coda: This portion, commencing in measure 160, is built over the tonic pedal with the exception of the last four bars. The fleeting moment in the key of A minor in measure 169 is very tasteful in its manner of delaying the final cadence. Three round and full "orchestral" chords conclude this exquisite movement.

THE LATE PERIOD

Sonata in C Minor (K. 457)[24]

This sonata is the grandest and most impassioned of all Mozart's piano sonatas. While it is charged with orchestral feeling, it is, withal, pure piano music.

---

24 Composed October 14, 1784, and dedicated to Mozart's pupil, Thérèse von Trattner, second wife of the printer and publisher, Johann Thomas von Trattner. It was published with the C Minor Fantasy (K. 475), May 20, 1785.

FIRST MOVEMENT *(Molto Allegro)*. The first movement is in sonata form.

Exposition—First Theme: The movement opens with a
Rakete ("rocket") figure. The motive rises in unison. In
metaphorical terms, this motive is fate making a searching
inquiry. It is maximum in its massiveness, although Mozart
does not indicate a double *forte* for it. The answer to the
Rakete figure is marked *piano,* not *pianissimo*—a point which
must be underlined. The beseeching quality of humanity's answer to fate is a most vital intangible which must be tonally
articulate. This answer accumulates intensity up to the A
flat in measure 4. The repetition of the question-and-
answer pattern is effected in the dominant. In this case,
however, it is again equally insistent and imploring. In
measure 9, a pedal point begins on the bass and is sustained
throughout measure 12 and half of measure 13. It is important to observe the *forte–piano* markings in both parts.
The upbeat to measure 10 initiates a chromatic descending
figure in the alto. Mozart used this chromatic figure as a
sorrow motive. With the last quarter of measure 11 the
same figure begins in the soprano. The very intense "Mannheim sigh"[25] is employed in the alto at this point, whereas
it is used in the soprano in measure 10.

In measure 17 there occurs a succession of downward
figures denoting resignation. The passage is marked *piano.*
This *piano* should commence on the G (second note in the
group of four eighths in the right hand), as the first note
of the measure, E flat, is a part of the preceding phrase,
and possesses its intensity. Measure 19 places the *Rakete*
figure an octave higher than the opening bar of the movement, thus preparing for an enormous leap from the E flat
in the right hand (second quarter, measure 20) to the same
figure starting on the B flat in measure 21. Measure 23

Tempo markings differ in the various editions: Schirmer—*Molto Allegro;*
Kalmus (Urtext)—*Allegro* (Autograph) and *Molto Allegro* (Artaria);
Breitkopf and Härtel—*Molto Allegro.*
[25] Suspension with the resolution down.

brings an episode in the relative major, and although it is marked *piano,* the tone must remain full and round. (This section cannot, any more than the remainder of the work, be played with a surface technique.) In the oldest Breitkopf and Härtel editions, there is no indication of *piano* in measure 30. With such an indication in many of the present editions, one may have an inclination to play this dialogue softly and sweetly. The two E flats rising to the B flat (last and first beat, measures 30–31, respectively) should be strident, culminating in measures 34–35; there should be an all but *imperceptible* retard on the second half of measure 35, with a diminuendo and a gentle "give" which flows into the second theme.

Second Theme: This section, in orchestral metaphor, is a masterful dialogue between the violins and the cellos. The different registers of the piano will create this effect if the performer is properly aware of the orchestral configuration. To give a figurative *explication de texte,* these different voices represent the feminine and the masculine, the sopranos and the basses. The unmistakable supplication written into the music by Mozart must be *read* into it by the performer. Without this feeling of hauntingly incessant wistfulness, the fundamental message is lost.

Suddenly (measure 44), there is an awakening! The half notes in the right hand are compressed into quarters in measure 45. This chromaticism upward with the contrary movement in the left hand is one of Mozart's most dramatic effects. The rest in measure 45 is extremely important. The player should remain immobile at this point, as any motion of the body would destroy the intensity. Measures 46–47 are a statement of resignation to destiny's disposition. The chromatic passage in measure 48 should make a crescendo to the thematic reaffirmation in measure 49. The triplet figure in measure 51 must be brilliantly clear, gaining in both intensity and volume up to and including the inverted E flat chord on the first beat of measure 57. No cessation of intensity should be considered until this chord is played. Then an ever-so-slight retard in the cadence into measure 59 is again apt. At this point, the insistent, pleading motive makes an upward thrust. The eighth rests are crucial. One must not overhold or pedal through these figures. With the beginning of the use of the trill in measure 63, we again see Mozart's achievement of intensification through ornament. The canonic treatment in 72 is amplified with the beseeching motive in the right hand, which brings the exposition to a close.

Development: This opens with the *Rakete* in C major. Only the first two measures remain in the major. The balance of the development is in "dark" minor. There is a perceptible note of the tragic in the reference to the second subject, in F minor, starting at measure 79. In measure 83, however, a furious encounter takes place, evocative of the spirit of a full orchestra. This emotional crisis is maintained until the rest in measure 94—all of this creating a strong mood of discontent and turmoil. (At this point, the performer ought to remain immobile to enhance the intensity of the mood.) At measure 94, there is an abrupt stop, followed by a *subito piano* in the falling fragments of the diminished chord. Finally there is a *pianissimo* resolution to the $V_{6/5}$ and the ensuing *fermata.* This development achieves a stirring effect. Not the least important factor contributing to this effect is Mozart's use of the diminished chord, to which, in many respects lamentably, modern ears have become desensitized. In Mozart's day, the diminished chord was much more dissonant than it is today.

Recapitulation: This is treated in precisely the same manner as the exposition. Measure 118 starts a momentary cannon, followed by a brief, romantic *cantabile* built around the Neapolitan sixth.

Coda: The coda begins in measure 169 with a canon, and the tonal curtain descends upon a scene of tragedy to which the spectator must be resigned (measures 177–182).

A murmur in the codetta (measures 183–184) brings the movement to a close with little, if any, retard.

SECOND MOVEMENT *(Adagio)*.   This *Adagio* is in rondo form. If the interpreter will count a slow eight, the tempo will be properly set. Warning must be issued, however, that unless there is a feeling of direction and movement, this slow tempo may result in dragging and disintegration of the movement. The tempo is also contingent upon the intensity with which one wishes to project the movement.

This section is elegaic—expressive of yearning and sorrow from the tragic opening statement. The opening tone of the melody, B flat, descends to F; thus, the downward motion produces the feeling of depression of spirits. The *sotto voce* in measure 1 and the *forte* in measure 2 are important in Mozart's basic conception. The turn beginning on the upper-note in the third quarter of measure 2 should be executed smoothly—not rushed—so as not to disturb the tranquility of the passage.

With the upbeat of measure 6, a figure is repeated three times. In the case of such obvious repetitions, the intensity must be established and heightened. This can be achieved through a slight but steady crescendo to the *forte* on the I_6 chord in the third quarter of the measure.

Repetition of notes or figures may have either or both of two functions: sustaining tone, and (more usual) building crescendo. The repeated E flat in measure 11, leading to the dissonant C sharp in the third quarter, succinctly and eloquently exemplifies such a crescendo. Beginning with the third quarter note in measure 13, there is a codetta which is the least intense passage in the movement.

One should bring out, avoiding the effect of belaboring, the hidden canon between the parts in measures 24–25. Mozart employs the *tirata*[26] in measures 29–30, thus disturbing the peaceful quality of an otherwise tranquil section. Very seldom did Mozart venture into remote devices—restraint

---

[26] A rapid run or scale passage usually starting with a turn.

being the keynote in this as it was in his selection of keys. For instance, in measure 32, G flat major is used for the start of the last half of this episode and for the beginning of a series of modulations in measures 34–37. These modulations are structured upon great emotional depths which increase in intensity to a large climax in the fourth quarter note of measure 37. After the first note G in the right hand of measure 38, there is a sudden *piano,* and the arpeggios, commencing on the pedal point G, form a murmuring retransition to the principal theme in measure 41.

THIRD MOVEMENT *(Molto allegro).*[27]   This movement is written in enlarged sonatine form.

First Theme: The movement begins with a soft, pleading passage which grows into a characteristic "fate" motive in the *forte* measure 16. The four measures beginning with measure 21 bear the semblance of full orchestral music. Every octave and chord should be accented in them. The descending seventh into measures 26–27 evokes another mood of Senecan resignation like the one in the exposition of the first theme.

Musicologists conjecture that Mozart intended an entrata in measure 45 on the dominant seventh chord.[28] Mozart himself more than likely used a short cadenza here; but, although some performers have tried to write out a passage, it seems less precarious to play the chord, with a hold, as edited today.

Second Theme: This begins in measure 47, is intended to be quiet, even with the supplicating seventh (B flat to A flat). Measures 74–76 have much in common with measures 59–61 in the first movement. Many editions have kept the left hand in a comfortable position regarding range in measures 93–100. But the intensity is greater if one follows the autograph (Urtext: Kalmus edition). There

---

[27] *Molto allegro* in the Autograph (Urtext: Kalmus edition); *Allegro assai* in Artaria, Schirmer, and Breitkopf-Härtel.

[28] This is also sometimes termed an *Eingang* ("entrance").

should be a massive crescendo to measure 103, then a complete silence, before returning to the original theme in measure 105. The D flat in measure 151 is called a *Klage* (literally, a "lament"). It adds to the intensification of the passage.

Mozart has written out the cadenza in measures 218–221 (inclusive). The *a piacere* section has been discussed earlier in the chapter on Mozart's choice of keys and chords.[29] Care must be exercised in using an appoggiatura of correct duration in measure 244, and a short appoggiatura in measure 246 at the *a tempo*.[30] A spirit of defiance permeates measures 294–310. Then, as if overwhelmed by the futility of either defiance or supplication, the melodic line trails to a defeated *pianissimo* in measure 318—where the last two chords remind us of the "fate," the destiny which has remained unfulfilled.

Sonata in B Flat Major (K. 570, 1789)

In contrast to the stormy and dramatic C Minor Sonata (K. 457), this sonata reflects a serene quality of childlike simplicity—the impressive simplicity of a great and mature artist.

Mozart has written in his own thematic catalogue of compositions that this sonata was originally written for the piano alone. To some editions, however, a violin part (probably also Mozart's) has been added.

FIRST MOVEMENT *(Allegro)*. This *Allegro* is written in sonata form.

Exposition—First Theme: The first theme arouses interest from the opening bar, if it is handled properly, i.e., in the correct tempo—which is all-important here. An examination of measures 35–40 shows that groups of sixteenth notes have replaced the eighths used to this point.

---

29 See page 28, Chapter Four.
30 The appoggiatura must be played *on* the beat—*never before it*—in Mozart.

Hence, the tempo gives the impression of being accelerated here. If these sixteenths are played crisply, yet not too hurriedly, a correct tempo may be established. The opening measures of the first theme may seem somewhat slow at this tempo, until the real meaning of the work is discovered—through a clear sense of directional execution and an inner intensity which derive, in part, from long hours of thoughtful devotion to Mozart's works. This movement is an excellent instance of a musical work which the musician is compelled to study and restudy in its entirety in order to arrive at a proper sense of proportion in setting tempos for the various parts within the whole. One is reminded of the importance of gaining insight *after* rather than previous to a given experience. This insight—an inner working knowledge of the composition—must be built on practice.

Although each measure is phrased independently in measures 1–4, the thematic line must be preserved by the use of *legato* and directional playing.[31]

The V_7 chord with its upbeat (measure 5) must be stressed sufficiently to sound through the two measures it occupies—to a calm resolution on the first beat of measure 7. Immediately the line rises again to join the upbeat to measure 9, where the V_7 chord, repeated, should be played with even greater intensity.

The pedal must be used judiciously at all times. Especially in measures 12–15, every rest must be observed. These measures can be played *mezzo-forte* to effect a contrast with the *piano* repetition in measures 16–20. The chords in measures 21–22 must be executed with utmost precision—in much the spirit or style of two vigorous downbows, if one thinks in terms of the violin.

The lovely transition theme in E flat (measures 23–34) must be played with warmth and intensity rising to the B flat, first beat in measure 25, from which the descending chromatic line diminishes. The diminished chord in measure

---

[31] "Directional playing": the movement toward a climax of the phrase.

28 possesses more dramatic power than the V₇ in measure 24, which contributes to a gradual building toward the forte and the intensified sixteenth notes in measures 35–39.

Second Theme: As in the last movement of the D Major Sonata (K. 576), Mozart uses figures from the first theme in order to create the second theme. It may be helpful interpretively for the performer to imagine the second theme scored for the cello, with a flute obligato entering in measure 43.

One should by no means overlook the powerful yet tender V₇ chord of G minor in measure 54. Although the passage beginning with measure 57 is marked *forte,* the student should give preference to the theme in the bass, which is a repetition of the same material as is used in the soprano in measures 49–54. Care must be exercised not to hurry the sixteenths in this passage, or those leading to the end of the exposition.

Development: The beginning is a sudden leap to D flat. The transition passage from the first theme to the second is transposed and modified. Then the second theme is developed. It appears in the key of G major in measure 101, and in C minor in measure 109; finally, it appears as a V₇ figure, going into F minor in measures 113–117. The figure accompanying the second theme is developed and extended. It finally leads to the V₇ chord of the tonic.

Recapitulation: This begins in measure 134 and is a repetition of the exposition, with the exception of the necessary chordal change in measures 163–170 to prepare for the return of the second theme in the tonic key.

Codetta: This, also, is a transposed repetition from the similar passage in the exposition, and ends the first movement.

SECOND MOVEMENT *(Adagio).* This is in the old rondo form. The rhythm of the movement should be in two-quarter, rather than four-quarter, time, although it is written in the latter. In this respect it forms a parallel with the slow movement of the C Minor Sonata (K. 457).

Principal Theme: The first four chords of the principal theme in the opening of this movement stimulate comparison with the beginning of the second movement in the "Les Adieux" Sonata (Op. 81a) of Beethoven. The orchestral effect is unmistakable. The intervals are written as if for horns. Arm weight can assist in producing a full, round tone to sustain this illusion. Measures 3–4 may suggest the wood winds in this "orchestra."

The performer should observe the accent indications in the latter half of measure 3. Giving these accents *portamento* touch would be in good taste in this tranquil passage. Eighteenth century phrasing demands that the small phrase in measure 5 end on the D (first sixteenth note of the fourth beat), and the succeeding notes form an upbeat to the next phrase in measure 6. The same phrasing should be observed in this measure. After the double bar (measure 12), the descending thirds in the minor theme will be enhanced in intensity if a slight extra pressure is given to the first beat of the measure. Emphasis also on the F sharp in the bass (measure 15) will point up the resolution to the following G. The sequential design in measure 19 will be rendered more effective if it is played somewhat more softly than the preceding measure. The dialogue in measures 26–27 after the double bar of measure 25 is highly tasteful, if interpreted faithfully.

The fresh theme commencing in measure 34 should be played with a full, round tone. This contrast will enhance the final return of the principal theme. The coda is built of thematic fragments. This movement ranks among the loveliest in Mozart's later piano sonatas.

THIRD MOVEMENT *(Allegretto).* Inasmuch as the thematic construction shows two complete short movements, each in ternary form and closing with a perfect cadence

in its own key, this section—a movement within a movement
—must be termed episodical, rather than rondo, in form.

The charm of this movement lies in its simplicity. Yet,
for all the apparent ease of writing, the performer has only
to scan the middle sections to find a wealth of counterpoint
hidden in the cloak of humorous composition.

Principal Theme: After phrasing the upbeat B flat to
the D in the treble (first measure), then this D and the following E flat should be played very staccato, if only because
of the rests. This treatment will bring to the principal
theme the lightness so necessary to its projection.

The ornament on the second quarter note of measure
8 should begin on the upper auxiliary in spite of its seeming
difficulty. If it is consoling to the performer, the old Breitkopf and Härtel edition omits this trill. Care must be
taken not to make this measure sound labored, should the
trill be played.

After the middle part of the chief section, built upon
rhythmical segments of the principal theme, a very slight
retard in measure 15 will enhance the return of the initial
subject in measure 16.

First Episode: An episodic theme—rather demanding
in quality—is introduced in measure 23. This effect can be
obtained by a slight accent and bounce on the first and third
beats of this measure. The succeeding measure (24) is a
tranquil resolution on the tonic pedal. The rhythmic pattern just discussed is carried into the D minor section of
measure 31. The demanding character changes to a more
pleading one briefly, after which the demand is made again
in measure 35.

Second Episode: Measures 43–44 form a humorous transition to the contrapuntal second episode beginning in measure 45. This entire section, up to the return of the original
theme in measure 63, is a good example of Mozart's delightful polyphonic invention.

Coda: A lengthy coda begins in measure 71, and employs

fragments from the demanding episode, as well as modified portions of the contrapuntal second episode. Although Mozart has indicated that the last measure should be played *forte,* this is relative to the dynamics of the last four bars, which are played *piano.*

Thus, an inspired and inspiring creation is brought to a close.

BIBLIOGRAPHY

ABERT, HERMANN. *W. A. Mozart.* Leipzig: Breitkopf and Härtel, 1923 (1st ed., 1919). 2 vols.

ALDRICH, PUTNAM. *Ornamentation in J. S. Bach's Organ Works.* New York: Coleman-Ross Co., Inc., 1950.

ANDERSON, EMILY. *Letters of Mozart and His Family.* London: Macmillan and Co., Ltd., 1938. 3 vols.

APEL, WILLI. *Masters of the Keyboard.* Cambridge, Mass.: Harvard University Press, 1947.

BACH, CARL PHILIPP EMANUEL. *Essay on the True Art of Playing Keyboard Instruments.* Tr. and ed. by William J. Mitchell. New York: W. W. Norton and Co., Inc., 1949.

BANISTER, HENRY C. *Lectures on Musical Analysis.* London: George Bell and Sons, Ltd., 1902.

BARRINGTON, DAINES. "Account of a Very Remarkable Young Musician." *Philosophical Transactions of the Royal Society,* Vol. XL. London: Nichols, 1770.

BLOM, ERIC. *Mozart.* New York: Pellegrini and Cudahy, Inc., 1949.

DANNREUTHER, EDWARD. *Musical Ornamentation.* London: Novello, Ewer and Co., 1893–95. 2 vols.

DAVENPORT, MARCIA. *Mozart.* New York: Charles Scribner's Sons, c1932.

DAVID, HANS, and MENDEL, ARTHUR. *The Bach Reader.* New York: W. W. Norton and Co., Inc., 1945.

DENT, EDWARD J. *Mozart's Operas.* London: Oxford University Press, 1947.

DUNHILL, THOMAS F. *Mozart's String Quartets.* London: Oxford University Press, 1927.

EINSTEIN, ALFRED. *Mozart—His Character, His Work.* New York: Oxford University Press, 1945.

FISHER, HENRY. *The Musical Examinee.* London: J. Curwen and Sons, Ltd., 1845.

GIRDLESTONE, C. M. *Mozart's Piano Concertos.* London: Cassell and Co., Ltd., 1948.

GOETSCHIUS, PERCY. *Lessons in Music Form*. Boston: Oliver Ditson, 1904.

GOODRICH, A. J. *Complete Musical Analysis*. Cincinnati: The John Church Co., 1889.

HADOW, SIR WILLIAM HENRY. *Sonata Form*. London: Novello, Ewer and Co., 1896.

HIPKINS, A. J. *A Description and History of the Pianoforte*. London: Novello, Ewer and Co., 1896.

HUTCHESON, ERNEST. *The Literature of the Piano*. New York: Alfred A. Knopf, Inc., 1948.

HUTCHINGS, ARTHUR. *A Companion to Mozart's Piano Concertos*. London: Oxford University Press, 1948.

JAHN, OTTO. *The Life of Mozart*. Tr. by Pauline D. Townsend. London: Novello, Ewer and Co., 1882. 3 vols.

KOCH, CASPAR. *The Organ Student's Gradus ad Parnassum*. New York: J. Fischer and Bro., 1945.

LANG, PAUL HENRY. *Music in Western Civilization*. New York: W. W. Norton and Co., Inc., 1941.

MACPHERESON, STEWART. *Form in Music*. London: J. Williams, 1930.

MARKS, F. HELENA. *The Sonata: Its Form and Meaning*. London: William Reeves, 1921.

MOZART, LEOPOLD. *A Treatise on the Fundamental Principles of Violin Playing*. Tr. by Editha Knocker, with a Preface by Alfred Einstein. London: Oxford University Press, 1948.

MURPHY, HOWARD A. *Form in Music for the Listener*. New York: Radio Corporation of America, 1945.

NIECKS, FREDERICK. *Dictionary of Musical Terms*. New York: G. Schirmer, n.d. (Preface, 1884).

PAUER, ERNST. *A Dictionary of Pianists and Composers for the Pianoforte, with an Appendix of Manufacturers*. London: Novello and Co., 1895.

SAINT-FOIX, GEORGES DE. *The Symphonies of Mozart*. New York: Alfred A. Knopf, Inc., 1949.

SHEDLOCK, J. S. *The Pianoforte Sonata*. London: Methuen and Co., Ltd., 1895.

TOBIN, J. RAYMOND. *Mozart and the Sonata Form*. London: William Reeves, 1916.

TURNER, W. J. *Mozart: The Man and His Works*. New York: Alfred A. Knopf, Inc., c1938.

WYZEWA, T. DE, and SAINT-FOIX, GEORGES DE. *W. A. Mozart*. Vols. I and II, Paris: Perrin et Cie., 1912; Vol. III, Paris: Desclée de Brouwer et Cie, 1936.